PRAISE FOR *TRIP TALES*

"Get ready for adventure and big laughs as author Rosanne S. McHenry regales you with tales of her coming-of-age during family camping trips up and down the western United States and Canada. *Trip Tales* continue when she gives readers numerous rare, up close, and unflinching views of the ups and downs of the life of a ranger—the job she was born to do."

—BARBARA L. MORITSCH
Ecologist
Author of *The Soul of Yosemite: Finding, Defending,
and Saving the Valley's Sacred Wild Nature*
and *Wolf Time*

"In Trip Tales, Rosanne McHenry displays her stellar storytelling skills as she takes us with her on her journey from hapless camper to rock star ranger. With humor and insight, she shares the lessons learned along the way as well as her deep and abiding love and respect for the land."

—DIANNE MILLIARD
National Park Ranger
Wrangell-St. Elias National Park and Preserve

"*Trip Tales* takes the reader through the author's family experiences that influenced her career choice as a park ranger. Well-written, it is entertaining while delivering a serious message on 'what it takes' to work in this field. A must-read for someone considering such a career, and a fun read for anyone."

—DENZIL VERARDO, PH.D.
Co-author of *The Sempervirens Story:*
A Century of Preserving the Redwoods
and former Chief Deputy Director, California State Park System

"A delightful tale of adventure in the great outdoors— from childhood camper to park ranger— a life joyously lived and charmingly told with heart and humor. Bravo!"

—JOANN LEVY
author of *Yosemite Farewell:*
An Untold Tale from the California Gold Rush
and *They Saw the Elephant: Women in the California Gold Rush*

"Rosanne's engaging stories of her family's vacations in our national and state parks are an inspiration to parents and teachers. Her adventures led to a fascination with nature and a career as a dedicated and passionate National Park Ranger."

—KITTY WILLIAMSON
Trip Leader, Sierra Club Inspiring Connections Outdoors
and Certified California Naturalist

"*Trip Tales* is a fun and enjoyable stroll down memory lane. I believe all readers who spent their childhoods camping with their families will relate fondly to the adventures and misadventures of the author, her siblings and her parents. As a retired California State Park Ranger, I especially enjoyed Ms. McHenry's recollections of her time working at Mt. Rainier. I look forward to reading the next installment of her memoir, *Trip Tales Two: Travels with Gus.*"

—SUSAN McLAUGHLIN
California Supervising State Park Peace Officer,
Ranger (Retired)

"The author and I met in unusual circumstances. We bumped into each other in a village in northern Lapland, well above the Arctic Circle. Each of us had been invited to a symposium to speak about gold in our representative countries. Rosanne is a remarkable woman and it is gratifying that she has agreed to commit aspects of this significant life of hers to print.

—DR. RONALD M. CALLENDER
Fellowship of the Royal Photographic Society
Author of *Gold in Britain*

"A fun and insightful read into the joys of being outdoors, and the trials and tribulations in the early life of a park ranger."

—MIKE LYNCH
California State Park Ranger, Historian,
and retired Ranger/Superintendent

"This is a remarkable book. I laughed. I cried. I now want to take my family camping after previously swearing that would be a bad idea. Rosanne McHenry depicts her own family with such tender affection and lucidity that you will fall in love with these delightful people and their raucous outdoor adventures. You'll also get to follow along as those very childhood experiences influence her to become a full-fledged interpretive park ranger caring for and sharing our nation's natural heritage. Her zeal for the rugged outdoor life—and her respect for its humbling dangers and grandeur—is positively contagious."

—GENEVIEVE PARKER HILL
Author, *Experience Over Stuff*

From Family Camping to Life as a Ranger

ROSANNE S. McHENRY

Huntley Avenue Press
Auburn, California

Trip Tales

From Family Camping to Life as a Ranger
Rosanne S. McHenry

Huntley Avenue Press
Auburn, California

www.TripTalesBook.com

This is a work of creative nonfiction based on the memories of the author. The conversations in the book are from the author's recollections and are not intended to represent word-for-word accuracy, but are told in a way that evokes the feelings and meanings of what was said. In all cases, the essence of the dialogue is accurate. In some case, names and identifying information may have been changed to protect privacy.

Editor: Heidi Eliason, www.HeidiEliason.com
Index: Russell Santana, www.E4Editorial.com
Cover and Interior Design: Yvonne Parks, www.PearCreative.ca

Library of Congress Control Number: 2021912925

Publisher's Cataloging-In-Publication Data
(Prepared by The Donohue Group, Inc.)

Names: McHenry, Rosanne S., author.
Title: Trip tales : from family camping to life as a ranger / Rosanne S. McHenry.
Description: Auburn, California : Huntley Avenue Press, [2021] | Includes index.
Identifiers: ISBN 9781737416203 (paperback) | ISBN 9781737416210 (Kindle) | ISBN 9781737416227 (ePub)
Subjects: LCSH: McHenry, Rosanne S.--Anecdotes. | Women park rangers--United States--Biography. | Outdoor recreation--Anecdotes. | Hiking--Anecdotes. | Wilderness areas--Anecdotes. | LCGFT: Autobiographies. | Anecdotes.
Classification: LCC GV191.52.M34 A3 2021 (print) | LCC GV191.52.M34 (ebook) | DDC 796.5092--dc23

Dedication

To my husband, Vernon, and our children, Cameron and Tristan. The best things that ever happened to me in life!

Contents

Foreword

Trip Tales, Rosanne McHenry's debut work is a refreshing twist on an unexpected autobiographical chronology. Influenced by the rugged self-sufficiency of her parents—her father was born and raised in the Santa Cruz Mountains of California and her mother immigrated from Italy—the author entertainingly takes the reader through outdoor experiences with her family. Those experiences led to the pursuit of a career as a park ranger. Filled with mirth and humor, *Trip Tales* would make a great "beach read" in and of itself. However, there is a more compelling reason to read this book.

Underlying the tales of camping with her family lies the lasting impression that those adventures in the outdoors made on the author. What she saw and learned on those trips, and the interactions that took place in the out-of-doors, she applied as a park ranger. People are human and make mistakes when enjoying the heritage that is our national and state parks, and McHenry's family was no exception. However, the author learned from those mistakes and approached the job of park ranger with compassion and humanitarianism. Her love of people is obvious, from her years camping with her family to her experiences as a park professional.

Rosanne McHenry's pursuit of a career as a national park ranger documents the difficulty of gaining entry into this highly desirable profession. She also had to break through the "glass ceiling" that existed in the male-dominated park service. But through all of the trials and tribulations involved in the pursuit of her "dream" job, her belief in the value of our parks and the enjoyment of those who use them was only strengthened.

Trip Tales is a fun read, but the deeper underlying current is the real prize for the reader. It is humorous, but also offers a serious introspective of a career as a park ranger—its joys, its internal politics, the blessings and burdens of being a uniformed civil servant. To a young group of school children, rangers may seem super-human. The author's experiences expose the fiction in that view by emphasizing the humanity that success in the profession demands.

Denzil Verardo, Ph.D.
Author and former Chief Deputy Director,
California State Parks

PREFACE
Family Beginnings

My father was born in the little village of Ben Lomond and was raised in the rugged Santa Cruz Mountains of California. As a child he gained a deep appreciation of nature, exploring ancient redwood groves and fishing sandy creeks in shadowy fern canyons. He loved being outside, especially in the forest.

My mom loved the ocean. She was an Italian immigrant, born in the tiny little village of Camigliano near Lucca in Northern Italy. She came to this country with my grandmother when she was one year old. My grandfather had arrived in the United States a year earlier to prepare a home for his family. They lived in East Chicago, Illinois; then in Oakdale, California; and finally in San Francisco.

My grandparents' house on a hill overlooking the San Francisco Sunset District was a wonder to visit, with sunlight streaming in through countless windows and a backyard filled with fresh-grown herbs of every variety. The aroma of that garden was heavenly.

My grandfather was a carpenter by trade, although he worked many different factory jobs to support his family. Strong and self-sufficient, he laughed easily.

My grandmother was the most amazing cook I've ever known. Holiday dinners were seven-course wonders with soup, homemade pasta, antipasto salad, and a huge main course with a roast and an array of colorful vegetables. These dinners were always followed by a dazzling assortment of desserts: chocolate torte, cakes, pies, cookies, fruit, nuts, and dessert wines. It's no wonder my mom always insisted on five-course meals, even on camping trips.

Holiday get-togethers were always great fun with my sister, brother, and our four cousins. We would run around, tear up the house, and misbehave at the kid's table during dinner. I laughed so hard at my cousins' antics that I often unwittingly snorted food right through my nose. Of course, we got yelled at by our parents, and it's no wonder it took many years for me to finally be allowed to sit at the grown-ups' table.

I miss those times.

Family picnics and camping trips were frequent outings as Mom and Dad took us to nearby lakes and beaches. In those days we only got a few channels on television. There was no internet, no cell phones, no video games, no streaming video, nor downloadable music. We only had small transistor radios with a few radio stations to listen to. If a family wanted to be entertained on the weekends, they went outside to the Great Outdoors.

We were always going on picnics in the woods or out to the beach. We often went to nearby lakes with cousins, aunts, uncles, and grandparents. Annual camping treks were something we looked forward to all year. My family didn't have money to go on trips to places like Hawaii or Europe. We could barely afford to rent a tiny little trailer and pay the campsite fees. I remember my mother saving pennies in a jar. But I wouldn't trade those times for a five-star hotel anywhere in the world. These trips were priceless beyond measure as we all reveled in the beauty of the outdoors.

Years later, after I grew up and moved away, I carried this love of nature with me. I became a national park ranger, then a California state park ranger, and finally a national park ranger again, my first and greatest love.

These are the stories of those funny mishaps and adventurous times. It is about what it meant to spend time together as a family in some of the most beautiful parks the West has to offer. These family adventures instilled a deep appreciation of nature in me, and the interactions with the park staff inspired me to become a park ranger.

I wanted others to read these stories and understand how important it is to go outside and appreciate the beauty of nature, and to experience our shared heritage on this beautiful planet, our Earth. This became my motivation for writing this book.

For each of you who dream of a favorite or funny outdoor experience anywhere in the world, I hope these stories will bring joy to your heart.

Rosanne Smith McHenry
April 2021

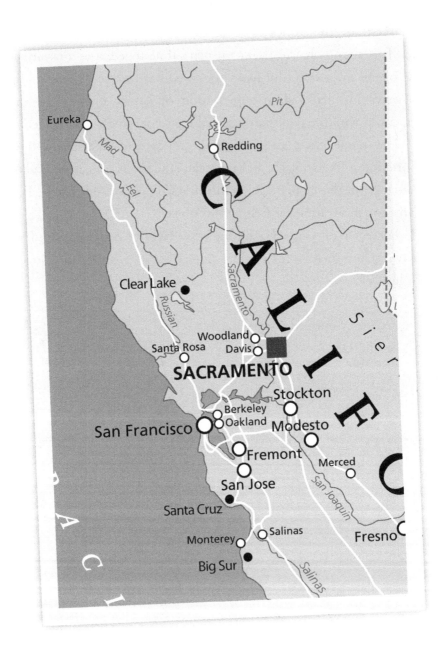

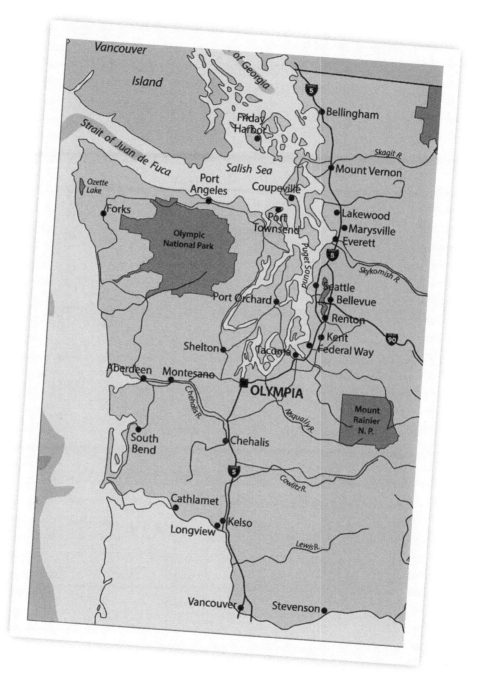

The Olympic Peninsula--shaded areas show locations of
Olympic National Park and Mount Rainier National Park

Olympic National Park highlighting the location of the Hoh Rain Forest

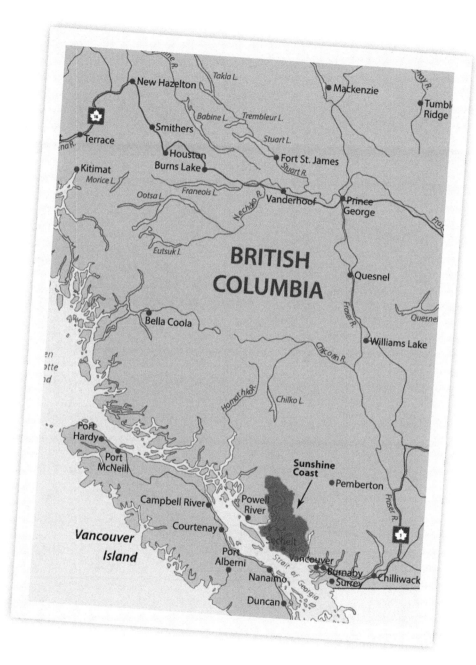

British Columbia--shaded area is the Sunshine Coast where we visited

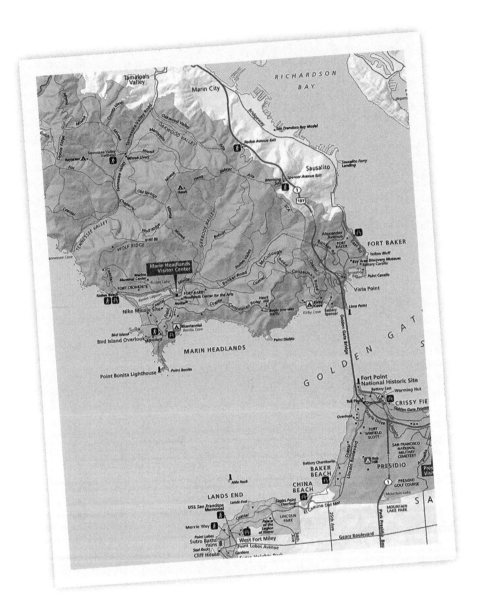

Marin Headlands section of the Golden Gate National Recreation Area—
the original park visitor center was at Rodeo Beach shown on the left

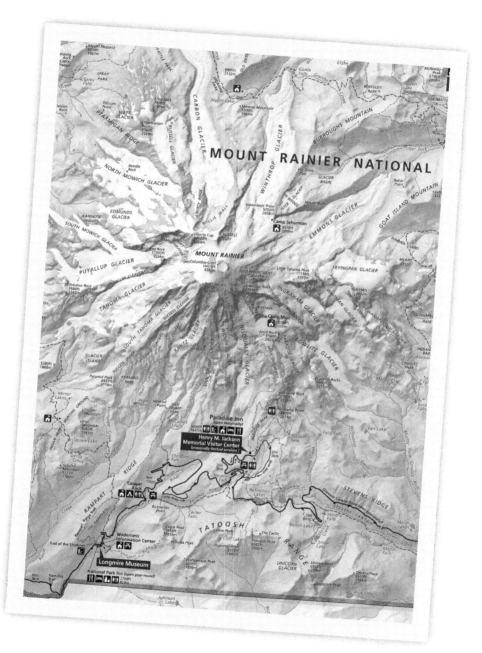

Mount Rainier National Park showing Longmire on the left

PART ONE

Family Camping
and
Outdoor Adventures

The Great Departure

"We leave at four a.m.!" My father's voice boomed across the dinner table. "Dress in your clothes and go to sleep on top of your beds. We're not wasting time getting dressed in the morning. There will be no bed-making. We'll be on the road no later than four a.m., so get to bed right after dinner and go to sleep."

"But Dad, it's only seven p.m.," we complained. "We want to watch TV."

"To bed!" he bellowed. "Tomorrow is the first day of vacation and we're not going to waste a single minute. Now go to bed, all of you, and get to sleep right now. We'll wake you up at three a.m."

It was 1964, and my dad got only one week of vacation per year, usually during the month of April. This meant we all got to miss school for a week. We did not mind this at all, even if we did have to do homework along the way. What kid hates leaving school for a week?

I was ten, my sister Nancy was five, and my little brother Gary was two. Six years later our baby sister, Chrisi, would join our family.

Dad rented a little teardrop trailer for our family each year for our annual camping trip. It was tiny for our family of five, but it was what they could afford. We all looked forward to this big and adventurous week away, camping on the California coast at Santa Cruz or Big Sur.

We were each given our own eight-by-eight-inch drawer in the trailer and were told to pack all the stuff we needed into it. One little drawer—it was hardly big enough to put socks in! But I grabbed two candy bars, two pairs each of socks and underwear, my favorite jeans, T-shirt, swimsuit, and shorts, and managed to stuff all of this into the tiny space. I was too young, or too much of a tomboy, to care about fashion.

"Remember to pack your toothbrush, Honey," my mom reminded each of us. Gary's drawer had Hot Wheels cars in it; he loved these.

It was a great time to be together as a family. We didn't have a lot of money, so my mom and dad saved spare change all year so we could buy little snacks on the trip. I loved getting this special allowance so I could buy barbecue potato chips and cream soda, things my mom wouldn't let us have the rest of the year. Nancy loved Junior Mints and gum, and usually got them both stuck in her hair. Gary loved food of any kind and would eat everything, everywhere if we didn't keep a close eye on him at all times.

Dad was larger than life, a big, burly, strong guy who loved his family. He stood six foot one and wore glasses and short-cropped hair. He looked like a big bear with light brown hair and hazel eyes. He loved the outdoors and took us on adventures whenever he could. Mom was a dark-haired, brown-eyed, Italian beauty with a soft voice and patient manner. Her thick, wavy hair and curvy figure turned heads wherever she went. She loved being with her family and cooking up big meals no matter where we went. Nancy was five years younger than me with a beautiful face; big, luminous brown eyes, and curly brown hair. Gary was seven years younger, a slim, blonde-headed, hazel-eyed boy who loved superheroes and wearing his Batman cape and utility belt. He could often be seen running around the neighborhood with his cape flying out behind him. I was a gangly-limbed, knobby-kneed tomboy with long brown hair who loved climbing trees, shooting slingshots, and riding boys' bikes. I scorned all things "girly." I loathed dolls, dresses, and fashion. I was happiest in a T-shirt and jeans.

True to his word, Dad woke us all up at three a.m. "Get up, get up! Time for vacation." We leaped up, fully clothed from on top of our neatly made beds, and stumbled downstairs to eat cold cereal. It tasted absolutely hideous in the middle of the night.

"Honey, couldn't we stop for breakfast?" my mother asked.

"No," my dad said. "We have a schedule to keep. If we leave right now, we should arrive there before eight a.m. and I can still go fishing this morning."

"But Dear, what's the rush?" Mom pleaded.

"Flora, you know we have only one week of vacation each year, and we are not going to waste a single minute of it here at the house, on the road, or at some damn restaurant. Now let's put these kids into the car and get on the road. No more questions. The camping trailer is all hooked up and the engine is running."

Never one to miss a meal, I gulped down my cereal. Nancy started crying, and Gary just sat there with a big, goofy grin on his face. I walked out to the car while Mom comforted Nan and settled my siblings into the back seat with me, covering us all with a ratty-looking blanket. Mom wearily clambered into the front seat. Dad put the car in drive, and we were off.

Each year we made a journey from our hometown of Pacifica, California, down Highway 1 toward Santa Cruz or Big Sur to camp for a week. This year it was Big Sur, the most beautiful stretch of coastline in the world.

We watched the sunrise as the car cruised along on the empty highway. It took four hours to wind our way along the rugged cliffs of Highway 1 through little coastal towns like Linda Mar, Montara, Half Moon Bay, Pescadero, San Gregorio, and on down to Santa Cruz, Monterey, Carmel, and Big Sur. The drive was beautiful, though, and I didn't mind. Dad got us each transistor radios to hold to our ears so we could listen to our favorite music.

I especially loved the section of road between Monterey and Big Sur. The coastline was spectacular where huge, sheer granite cliffs plunged straight down into the constantly churning, brilliantly aquamarine ocean. Rainbow-shaped bridges crisscrossed over steep creek canyons along the way, including the famous Bixby Creek Bridge, a magnificent span thirteen miles south of the village of Carmel. Redwood trees pierced the sky and cobblestone creeks washed into the surf. In some places, waterfalls cascaded straight down into the ocean.

My dad loved the campground at Pfeiffer Big Sur State Park. Back then it was undiscovered country, this beautiful, peaceful river valley on the coast. The soft, green redwood forest offered a welcome respite from our suburban life, and we loved the sound of the Big Sur River coursing right through the heart of the park. It was just a short drive from this valley out to the spectacular Big Sur coastline.

My dad had his favorite campsite scoped out, one where he could easily walk to the creek to fish, and right next to the restroom so that my mom could easily take Nancy to the toilet at night. I never understood why Nan had to use the restroom so much, but she did.

Check-in time was eleven a.m., but my father paid no heed to this. Nor did he give a damn about the sanctitude of the current campsite occupants. It was *his* chosen site; he had reserved it *specifically* for us, and it made no difference if the occupants were enjoying their final morning breakfast before departure, sitting quietly at their picnic table under the trees. Those poor people!

Dad would pull up right alongside the site, gun the engine while unleashing the full horsepower of our Plymouth Fury II, glare at the campers, and will them to leave. At first this incredible audacity had no effect, but eventually the frightened campers looked into the eyes of this madman, unsure of what he might do, as he blasted loud music over the car radio at full volume. Then they hurriedly packed up their belongings and fled.

I was horrified. "Dad, we can go wait in the picnic area," I said.

"Yes, Honey, there is no need to rush those campers out of their site," Mom offered. But Dad was not to be deterred.

Those poor people, I thought again. Good grief! I shrank way down in my seat, trying hard to hide from view. I felt like an idiot, a usurper, as the dispossessed campers fled in fear. But I was helpless to change the situation.

"ABOUT TIME!" my dad said, as he triumphantly backed into *his* campsite.

I watched as the previous occupants drove over to the picnic area on the other side of the river. They quietly set up their breakfast again at one of the picnic tables. Seemingly unruffled by their forced evacuation, they were soon talking and enjoying their breakfast again. Amazing. What a nice, peaceful family, I thought. I still felt like a jackass because we had disrupted them, but they seemed happy enough.

"Rosanne, help your sister and brother out of the car while I set up the trailer," Dad told me.

"Okay, Dad," I answered.

We poured out of the car, happy to be in the redwoods. Sunlight filtered down through the trees. Sounds were hushed in the cathedral groves of the forest. Sword ferns glistened from the morning dew and scrub jays chattered all around us, flitting from tree to tree. The creek rustled past with sunlight glinting off the water, beckoning us to wade in.

The campsites were large and comfortable, with picnic tables, grills, and wooden lockers to store food. We all took off in separate directions. I ran down to the swimming hole to check if it was still the way I remembered it from last year, a deep emerald pool with a giant granite boulder you could jump off of. Nan dragged Mom off to the restroom, and Gary stood there watching Dad. It had been a long drive and we were all glad to be out of the car. We couldn't wait to begin our week.

Nancy, Mom, Gary and me at Big Sur State Park

The Great
Displacement

Our little fourteen-foot-long trailer was very simply designed. It had a drop-down leg that supported the back end. It was simple enough in theory: back into your site, situate your rig, drop the back leg down, and settle the trailer into place. Remember to put the locking clamp down to give the back leg stability to support weight inside the trailer. My dad remembered every step—almost.

The interior was basic: a queen-size bed on the back end, a small kitchenette with a sink and propane stove in the center; a small dinette, which made into a bed on the opposite end; and a drop-down double bed above the dinette. Nan and I shared the upper bunk, Gary had the little dinette bed below, and Mom and Dad enjoyed the queen-size bed.

We had an enjoyable first day of camping. We went swimming, fishing, hiking, and bike riding—generally playing and having a good time.

That evening Mom made the first of a series of five-course dinners. When most families camped they fixed simple, one-skillet meals like macaroni and cheese, Hamburger Helper, or hot dogs on buns, and they served them on paper plates. Not my mom. Every meal had to be a complete five-course repast involving hours of preparation, followed by extensive cleanup.

"Mom," I said, "why do we have to make all this food for dinner? Why don't we just have hot dogs or something easy?" I had to help clean all the dishes, so I longed for a one-skillet meal.

"Rosanne, stop complaining and eat your dinner!" Dad ordered.

Dinner nearly always consisted of a soup or salad, a main course with meat, two vegetables, rice or potatoes, and bread with butter, followed by dessert and coffee. This meant that multiple skillets, pots, pans, plates, glasses, cups, and utensils needed to be extracted from cabinets and drawers, washed and dried after we ate, and neatly returned in place. I wondered how Mom could relax with all this food to cook, but she was Italian and so she lived for this. She even kept a little diary of what we all had eaten every day, including snacks.

So, while most happy families had finished their macaroni dinners on paper plates and gathered round the campfire hours earlier, we were busy washing, cleaning, drying, and putting away a mountain of dishes and then—well, by then it was almost time to prepare for bed.

Sleeping bags would have been a great idea—simply unroll your assigned bag and climb into it. But no! We had to make up complete beds for the night. Out came the sheets, blankets, pillows, coverlets, and bedspreads dragged from home, and we made up separate beds for each of us. I felt like a porter on a Pullman train car doing all this preparation. What a chore!

After dinner, Dad built a campfire. We roasted marshmallows and watched raccoons come into camp with their greedy little eyes reflecting the dancing firelight.

"Wonder what they eat?" I asked, ever the aspiring naturalist and future park ranger. Somehow my dad got the idea of feeding them the marshmallows. We were so dumb, having no idea that this could make them sick. We just thought it was a wonderful life-enriching experience, interacting with the local wildlife.

At first we just tossed them the marshmallows, but soon they closed in on us in a circle and we were feeding them right out of our hands. Where did they all come from, we wondered. We laughed when they reached out with their tiny, hand-like paws to snatch this human contraband from our grasp. Oh, what a joy to be exchanging such bonhomie with the local night creatures! Surely no other family had come up with such a clever idea. We were so amazing.

"Here, Honey, just hold the marshmallow out in your hand," Dad told us. "See? They won't hurt you. Aren't they cute? This is great, isn't it? Look how they come right up to us."

Nancy was having none of this. She slowly backed away, her eyes wide in terror, not trusting these scary, strange creatures for one single second. She even started crying when they came close. Smart girl.

Suddenly, our peaceful exchange was shattered by a loud cry. "OUCH, DAMMIT!" yelled my dad, as one of the bigger raccoons predictably bit deeply into his finger. "You little bastards!" he screamed in outrage, affronted that his human kindness had been completely betrayed by these furry, striped monsters. This sent the raccoon group scrambling for cover, tumbling over one another to get away from the screaming madman. "You better run, you little jerks!" he shouted. "Dammit, Flora, what the HELL?" My dad looked to my mom for solace.

"Oh Honey, your finger is bleeding," she said.

"I know it, Flora. Dammit! Get the iodine."

We all looked on in horror as my dad's thumb bled profusely, wondering if he would get rabies and die. Then the raccoons began a new advance upon us, looking for more marshmallows.

"Get outta here, you rotten devils!" Dad screamed, as he chased every last one back into the bushes. "Time for bed," he said, as he rapidly ushered us all inside the trailer, thereby bringing an abrupt end to our pure nature experience in the wild.

Later that night we were all snuggled into our beds, sound asleep, dreaming of redwood trees, feathery green ferns, fishing in clear running creeks, and swimming in sunshine. Suddenly, the quiet night was ripped apart with a great rending CRRRRAASH! The whole trailer had collapsed as the unsecured exterior support leg crumpled beneath us. My father had neglected to lock the exterior leg into place when he set things up that morning. My sister and I were catapulted out of our bunk onto the floor.

"What the HELL!" my dad hollered.

"Honey, be quiet; you'll wake the kids up," Mom said.

"Dammit, Flora, the kids are all over the floor!" he shouted.

Dad and Mom scrambled to pull themselves up against gravity to claw their way to the door. As the weight shifted the trailer crashed back into the horizontal position, and my dad flew out the front door. Cursing under his breath, he stomped around outside until he located the errant support leg and slammed it back into place. My mom stood there with a flashlight to make sure he carefully secured the locking clamp to avoid future catastrophes. We all came outside to witness the spectacle. My father herded us back into the trailer.

"It's okay, kids," he told us. "Everyone back into bed now; the trailer won't fall again."

The whole situation struck us kids as extremely funny. Nancy was snickering, and Gary was fascinated. Then we all went to bed, wondering if we would survive the "gravity" of the situation. Soon I could hear Dad snoring again, and I knew all was well. I fell into a deep and happy sleep, dreaming of catapulting far and wide over mountains and into the sea.

The next morning brought new adventures. My dad loved to fish. He would get up at four a.m. to be sure to catch the biggest and best fish. This was fine, but he also loved his morning coffee. He would put the percolator on, perk his coffee, and then pour himself a giant cup to drink. My dad did not simply drink coffee, he slurped it loudly, with great zest and zeal. He stood right next to my bunk, at eye level with my head, and with a loud SLUUURRP, he woke me up from a sound, and at this point, much-needed sleep.

"Dad, you woke me up," I whispered.

"Quiet, Rosanne, you're going to wake everybody up," he sternly replied. And again, SLUUURRRRP!

"Dad, please stop slurping your coffee!"

"Quiet, Rose. I told you to be quiet," he warned.

Then my Mom joined the chorus. "Honey, your slurping is waking us all up; will you please go outside?"

By now, Nancy was awake and started crying, "I wanna go to the bathroom!"

"Oh, for Pete's sake, I'm leaving," Dad said, as he stomped off, leaving my poor mom with a trailerful of upset children to coax back to sleep in the dark of the night.

Later that morning, Dad triumphantly returned at breakfast time with a string of fresh trout to cook.

"Ugh," Nancy and I said. "Who'd wanna eat those slimy things?"

"You just wait," he told us. "Fresh trout for breakfast!"

"Honey, not for breakfast, let's save them for dinner," Mom said, leaving us to our much-preferred box cereal. What a savior! Disappointed, Dad put the scaly monsters to bed in a cooler for the time being.

When Gary grew a bit older and learned to fish, my dad would take him out in the boat with him, or they fished together in the stream. Gary always came back with a string of fish, while Dad had only one or two. Every time!

"What is your secret?" I asked Gary.

He just smiled and said, "I have the will, and I will the fish to come to me."

Hmmm, I thought. This seemed to work later on with girls, too, as innumerable young women showed up on our doorstep looking for Gary. I guess he just willed them to come too.

Later that day I filled up an air raft and floated lazily along the creek near the swimming hole. I really enjoyed this drifting along, while watching the creek bottom flow underneath. I loved looking at all the brightly-colored pebbles and the shadow effect of the ferns in the water as I glided silently past.

It was just a short stretch of water, and I would float down, get out, walk upstream, and then float back down again. I loved the feel of the warm sun on my back. I was happily engaged in this activity when all of a sudden there were four fishing lines in the water in front of me. "Plop! Plop! Plop! Plop!" Several fishermen had waited for me to step out, and before I could get back into the water, they had dropped their lines in and taken over the entire area. I was devastated. This wasn't fair! I had arrived first. I had looked forward to being here all year.

My dad came along to check on me and, seeing my distress, he wasted no time in lambasting the errant fishermen. "What do you think you're doing, throwing your lines in the water to fish when my daughter was here first?" he bellowed. "You have no right! You should have waited until later. She was swimming here!" But he was ignored. It was four to one.

I told him, "It's alright, Dad." Secretly, I was lying, but I was very impressed with him defending me and trying to be my hero. He grumbled and cursed under his breath, but he decided it was a losing battle.

He put his arm across my shoulders and we walked back to camp together. He showed me how to clean the fish for dinner. At first, I was horribly disgusted from the look and the smell of the fish guts. It was gross. Yecchhh! All that quivering, multi-colored, foul-smelling goop! But Dad kept telling me how delicious the fresh trout would taste, fried in butter over the campfire. I watched and even helped him clean up afterward. He seemed so happy.

Dad worked really hard all year long, and this was his one week to enjoy time in the outdoors with his family. He was childlike in his joy of being outdoors in the warm, sunny weather. Our home was in the gray, dense, dripping, fog-shrouded area of Pacifica's Skyline Ridge, about ten miles south of San Francisco. It had to be the foggiest place on Earth. Seeing sunshine all day was a novel thing for us. We reveled in it.

I wondered how Mom could enjoy herself, taking care of a family of five in a tiny little trailer. But she told me she really loved it. I think maybe she was lying. She wore a leopard-skin print robe and furry slippers every morning. She loved that robe, and camping gave her an excuse to wear it through much of the day. She looked adorable.

That evening, true to his word, my dad fried the fish for dinner.

"I don't wanna eat those things!" Nancy cried. She was horrified and made all kinds of faces at "those stupid fish," so my mom fixed her some chicken. Gary and I were game, though. And the fish were delicious, just like Dad said. Nancy really missed out, but she didn't care. She figured we were all fools.

Mom waving from our trailer at Big Sur State Park

Me feeding raccoons. I soon realized this was NOT a good idea.

Mom with a hungry raccoon

Roasting Marshmallows

Many evenings we would sit around the campfire roasting marshmallows. Dad would forage around, tearing twigs off trees like a rampant bear gathering hibernation materials for the winter, until he had a great big, heaping pile on the ground. Then, he would proudly pull his trusty pocket knife out of his pocket and neatly trim the twigs free of any side shoots.

This method of pillaging the forest, like so many 1960s campers were wont to do back then, kept any new growth from happening. And, undoubtedly, some of these branches may have been poison oak during its dormant stages, which likely led to my siblings' distress when they later acquired rashes like lepers. Yet twigs were ripped from the forest, nonetheless, leaving devastation in the wake of it all.

After clearing the twigs of side branches, my father honed the tips into fine points so they could be used to impale unsuspecting marshmallows for eventual incineration in the campfire. We had to be careful not to unwittingly pierce our cheeks or tongues on these finely sharpened sticks. Sometimes we tried to use the sticks to impale each other, but usually Mom brought this type of foul play to a hasty end.

"Do NOT stab each other with your marshmallow sticks!" she cried out in distress. "Carroll, make the kids be more careful!" she implored.

"Rosanne and Gary, put those down!" Dad hollered. "We have to wait for the fire to get hot enough."

"How hot does it need to be, Honey?" Mom asked. "We don't want the kids to burn themselves!"

"Flora, relax! I'm just building the flames up a little," Dad said, as he tossed piles and piles of dried wood onto the fire without considering the potential consequences.

Suddenly and without warning, flames roared high into the air, turning night into day, and threatening to ignite the overhead trees. "Yikes!" Dad screamed as he reached for a blanket to quell the conflagration, nearly turning the campsite into a disaster zone. He managed to calm the flames, and we rushed to stomp out all the sparks.

Dad was a campfire connoisseur, and he did not like his marshmallows over-roasted, so he took great care in showing us how to gently brown them to caramelized perfection on all sides, turning them patiently and carefully so they were crusty on the outside and gooey inside, like crème brûlée on a stick. This took a tremendous amount of patience and skill. But my sister, and particularly my brother, loved letting them catch fire and turning them into red hot smoke bombs, which would furiously flame into mini-infernos.

Then Gary got the idea of combining all our sticks together into incendiary globs. These morphed into super smoke bombs that burst into multi-colored flames above the fire. The resulting fireworks, while transitory, were impressive. Unfortunately, this had the unintentional effect of igniting the overhanging branches of the surrounding shrubs, and pretty soon our campsite was on fire again.

"Dammit, dammit, dammit!" Dad screamed, as poor Mom ran inside our trailer to get pots of water to throw on the bushes. "What the hell just happened?" Dad shouted, as our happy family time deteriorated into a frenzied fire management episode with sparks flying in all directions. Every one of us jumped up to put out the rapidly spreading flames. Eventually, the blaze was doused. Our once-jovial campfire lay there in sad and sodden ruins.

"Jeez! What the heck is wrong with you kids?" Dad shouted. "Are you trying to burn the whole place down? Don't you realize what could have happened? You almost set the entire forest on fire! Everyone go to bed right now!" We all darted into the trailer to hide in our respective little bunks.

Later we could hear Mom's sweet, soft voice outside saying, "Honey, don't get so upset. Your stick was on fire too."

"I don't need a lecture, Flora," Dad said. "I just wish the kids would listen! Why do things always have to get so out of control?" He was really shouting at himself, though, because this was all his idea, and he knew it.

"I'll make some coffee and we can have some cookies," Mom said. This was often her solution to things, coffee and dessert. Soon we could hear the rustle of a package of Oreo cookies being opened, followed by pensive crunching and coffee slurping noises outside our window as Dad settled down, happily pacified by Mom's tender ministrations.

We got into our beds listening to their soft, muffled laughter as they recounted the incident together. Should we ask for some cookies? we wondered. Better not, we decided. Best to be good and go to sleep quietly. It had been a big day, and all was now well with the world. We fell asleep listening to the sound of cookie crunching and crickets chirping. Somewhere in the distance an owl hooted goodnight.

The Ice Cream Scoop Tragedy

The next day, we headed into town to get some groceries. Gary wanted ice cream, so Mom bought him a vanilla cone. "Do you want some, girls?" Mom asked.

"Ugh!" Nancy and I chorused. We were sick of the stuff. Dad drove a dairy truck for a living and he brought home tons of ice cream all the time. Our freezer was filled with an array that would make a supermarket manager jealous. Dad went out and bought a full-sized standing freezer for the garage and jammed this with even more ice cream. It was ridiculous, really. I never imagined a route driver was entitled to such a bounty. He probably wasn't, but that didn't stop Dad from bringing home even more. Hard to imagine kids being tired of ice cream, but we were.

But Gary lived for it. He was little and the experience was still new to him. He was happy; he had an ice cream cone in his hand as we climbed back into the car and drove to our campsite.

Then, the great American tragedy struck. Gary stepped out of the car into our campsite and his ice cream scoop slopped off the cone and onto the pavement. "WHAAAAAA!" he cried. "I want my ice cream!"

"Oh, for crying out loud, Gary," Dad sighed in exasperation. "Why didn't you eat that on the way home?"

"I was saving it!" Gary cried.

"Honey, can you please take him back to the ice cream parlor and get him another cone?" Mom implored, as Gary had now worked himself up into a frenzy of tears, holding his empty cone in his hand. Remnant ice cream drips were splotched all over his clothes.

"I want my ice cream!" he kept sobbing. Nancy and I looked at him in disdain.

What a dope, we thought. But I also thought he was incredibly cute with his little blonde head and hazel eyes.

"Oh, for Chrissake! Get back in the car, Gary. Flora, take that empty cone out of his hands! And let's get him wiped off. Geez!" Dad exclaimed. Gary was still crying as they drove off together, my dad wearing a totally exasperated look on his face. I could hear my brother crying all the way down the road. Nancy and I snickered at the absurdity of the whole thing.

But later they came back looking much happier. Gary and Dad sat in the ice cream parlor so Gary could eat his cone there. Dad decided to join him and had a banana split. We felt jealous because they looked so elated when they came back. We were left out, even though we had opted out earlier. Now who was stupid? Gary had gotten Dad all to himself and they had fun without us. Not fair! Hmmmm, I thought. He has already figured out how to work Mom and Dad. Nice trick. And he was only two years old! Crafty little devil.

Poison Oak!

In the years that followed, we made many trips down the coast to Big Sur and Santa Cruz, California. Camping trips can bring great joy, but they can also come with some major challenges. Sometimes our trips ended abruptly because of a disaster. One year, when he was maybe six years old, Gary got a landmark case of poison oak while we were staying at Big Sur.

Mom was Italian and Dad was German and Irish. I inherited my Mom's Mediterranean, olive-toned complexion, but Nancy and Gary were fairer. Especially Gary, who was—and still is—a blonde. I could run through poison oak and maybe get a few little spots, but Nan and Gary were different. Nan's skin would break out in angry boils even if the plant was a mile away, and Gary got poison oak rashes like a diseased leper.

Of course, all three of us went crashing through the forest like idiots, playing hide-and-seek, tag, and climbing up and down trees. We all got poison oak.

But Gary got a *whopper* of a case. The poor kid had it everywhere, but the worst spot was right between his legs. Yes, right *there*. His skin broke out into a mass of sores, and he was covered with the worst-looking, oozing, purplish-red rash I had ever seen. He writhed on the floor as my mom tried to apply ointment all over him. I heard the soft kawhissshhhh of the aerosol spray, saw him painted pink and white with the medication, and doubled over laughing. Gary didn't think it was so funny.

"Rosanne, go outside! You're not helping," Mom told me. "It's hard enough without you making him feel even worse!"

I laughed because it all looked and sounded so funny. But I seriously felt so bad for him. It really was awful, and I could only imagine how terrible it was for him. No one should have to go through that. It's a wonder he didn't go sterile instead of becoming the father of three strong and healthy boys many years later.

Gary still remembers this time with agonizing clarity. It was so bad that Dad and Mom had to take him to a local emergency room for a steroid shot. His eyes had swollen completely shut, all puffed out and alien-looking. He was in bed for over a week before he could fully open his eyes again. I looked at him lying there and gasped in horror. He looked like a swamp monster. He was unrecognizable. It was that bad. The poor kid! I felt awful for laughing earlier. I stayed by his bed to help care for him.

It had to be one of the worst cases in history. It took weeks for the swelling to completely subside and the rash to go away, but eventually he looked more human. I'm still not sure how my poor little brother lived through this trauma.

This whole incident reminded me of a time when I was the one who was suffering.

Rosanus Pucanus

In 1963 when I was nine years old, we went on a camping trip to Sunset Beach on the Santa Cruz coast. Somehow, I came down with the flu on our second day out. It was not just *any* flu, it had to be one of the worst cases in my life!

I felt so sick, I was helpless. I was miserable. Waves of nausea washed over me without end. My head was swimming in a queasy tide of misery. I could not stop vomiting. I wanted to die as I retched again and again. My insides roiled. I had horrible, angry, uncontrollable diarrhea. Death would have been welcome!

I felt terrible about the situation. My poor parents looked forward to this trip every year, and here I was ruining it. I was so ill that, to this day, I can still remember everything with absolute clarity.

At first, we all hoped it was just a twenty-four-hour flu (another name for food poisoning) and that it would subside. But my condition only got worse and worse, until it was obvious that I was not going to recover quickly.

Mom and Dad were worried that I would become dehydrated. They followed the popular (and abhorrent) task of giving enemas to reduce fever, but how do you effectively do this in a tiny little camp trailer? Eventually they realized it was hopeless. We would have to pack up camp and go home.

For those who may not have experienced one, an enema is a dastardly procedure that was quite popular in the 1960s as a way to reduce fevers in children. You put a towel down in the bathtub, laid your sick kid on this, and proceeded to impale their rear end with a long, hard plastic tube attached to a water bag. The water bag was squeezed and water was forced upwards into the colon to rehydrate the person. This took several rounds. To describe this procedure as brutal would be an understatement. Then you placed the child onto the toilet so they could release the pent-up water through runny bowel movements. What criminal mind ever thought of such a cruel procedure?

Supposedly, this rehydration process lowered the fever. It generally worked, but it was also quite traumatizing for the child. Thankfully, there was no way to give me an enema inside of a moving vehicle as we wound our way back up the Pacific Coast Highway.

After only a mile of me being in the car it became apparent that a different mode of travel would have to be employed. There was no way to stanch the flow of vomiting and diarrhea.

They took me to see a doctor in a little nearby town, but I was much too sick to get out of the car. A nurse came out to look at me and she was quite concerned. "She should not be traveling," she told my mom. But what were they supposed to do? I was much too sick to stay in camp. I had to get home. We could have gone to a motel, I guess, but my parents decided it would be best to get home as quickly as possible so I could rest.

In desperation, they decided to put me to bed in the trailer with my mom, while my dad drove slowly and carefully up the road toward home with my siblings in the car. Poor Mom! I was spewing like an angry volcano! She didn't know which end to hold the bucket up to. She would position the bucket at my mouth and then things would erupt at the other end. By some miracle she seemed deft enough to capture all the effluent as she swung the bucket back and forth. If I were the mom, I think I would have killed myself. She had incredible courage.

At one point during this tortuous journey my dad stopped to see how we were doing. Mom stepped out to see how my little sister and brother were faring.

"How come Rosanne gets to ride in the trailer? I wanna ride in the trailer!" Nancy cried. Mom looked at Dad in silent appeal to rescue her from the moment. He came into the trailer while Mom comforted Nancy and Gary in the car. Dad decided to try telling me a story to calm things down. He patted my head softly as he told me the ridiculous tale.

"You know," he said, "it's not every little girl who gets a disgusting flower named after her," he said.

"My name's not disgusting," I replied, somewhat indignant. "You and Mom named me Rosanne."

"That's not what I meant," Dad said. "I'm talking about this really disgusting flower. It's called a *Rosanus pucanus*. That's its scientific name."

Now I was intrigued. I loved science, even as a dorky little kid. "In that place on the ground back at our campsite, where you puked," Dad said, "each year a beautiful flower will grow, and it will open its petals wide on the first day of spring. It will be all the colors of puke: yellow, green, red, brown—"

"Stop, Dad, you're making me sick," I said. But he kept telling the story.

"Each year, this beautiful and delicate flower will open up wide. It will slowly reach up to the sky and then it will lean over and grunt loudly in a plant voice. It will say, "BLEAGGGHHHHH!" It will smell horrible too. And this will happen every year, right on the spot where you threw up."

I couldn't help but laugh. I was intrigued with the idea. I pictured that disgusting flower in my fevered head.

"Yup, they'll call that flower the *Rosanus pucanus*," Dad said. "People will come from all over the world just to watch it open. And if you can stop puking on the rest of the trip home, I will plant a special flower bulb in our garden just for you, and that's what we'll name it." Well, somehow that story worked. I kept thinking about that awful flower and I quit puking and pooping for the rest of the trip home.

This episode is indelibly printed on my brain. I felt so bad about it all. The long, sinuous ride home was torture. It seemed endless. We all felt exhausted hours later as we pulled up to our house. I was trundled off to bed to recover as my siblings cried out about the lost vacation. Dad took them out for ice cream and candy. This made them happy.

That week actually turned out to be a very good one, because my folks were able to get a lot of things done at home and relax in the absence of work responsibilities. We spent quiet time with each other in the comfort of our home, talking and laughing. I recovered after a few days. Even though we missed the beach, no one seemed to mind too much. Mom told me years later that she really enjoyed that special time of having everyone together at home. So gradually I let go of my Catholic guilt over the whole incident.

But the *Rosanus pucanus* flower blooms every year in the same spot at Sunset Beach, a beautiful, big, multi-colored, horribly smelling flower that opens up and says, "BLEAAAGGGHHHH!!!"

Time with Dad

We were on a family camping trip in 1965, and I was eleven. It was a sunny afternoon at New Brighton State Beach on the Santa Cruz coast. This is a lovely evergreen park on a long strip of beach with a campground and picnic area. We could camp in the shelter of pine trees and walk right down a path to the beach. At night we could hear the crashing of the waves as we drifted off to sleep. It was an altogether wonderful place to stay.

When I was a kid I rarely got to play with my dad. He went to work, and when he came home, he liked to read the paper, enjoy family time at dinner, and then watch television like many other fathers. He often worked multiple jobs to earn enough money for our family to live on. So, when we went camping, it was our big chance to hang out together and play outdoors. I loved this. He made family time so fun.

Both Mom and Dad loved the ocean. Dad had grown up in the Santa Cruz area, and Mom had lived in and around San Francisco before she met him. We often made trips to the beach no matter what kind of weather it was.

There was plenty of room to play and there were lots of trees with strong branches to climb. I loved to climb high up into the trees and could easily get forty to sixty feet off the ground in minutes.

"Rosanne, where are you?" Mom called.

"I'm up here, Mom," I cried, and she ran over to the base of the tree and looked around in confusion. I laughed as she looked up in alarm at me hanging high up in the canopy like a monkey.

Me, my little sister Nancy, and Dad

"What are you doing way up there? Are you trying to scare me? Come down!" she told me. So I would scamper down and look for someone to play with.

We were camped there for the week and, one day, Dad and I were outside just bouncing around a big ball together. It was great to have the time with him because he was always so busy at home. But little Nancy was looking on with a scowl. Dad was paying attention to me. She was sitting on the sidelines because she didn't want to play ball anymore. She wanted Dad to take her on a walk. Or she wanted me to play with her. Or maybe it was just pure jealousy that stole into her little heart that day. Who knows? She stood up and sauntered over to him with a long, sad face. Concerned, Dad stopped our ball game, and bent down to Nan so she could whisper in his ear.

"What's wrong, Sweetie?" he asked.

"Rosanne said a bad word, Daddy. She said dammit!"

My father's eyes grew wide. "She did?"

Nancy nodded her little head in affirmation. This was a total lie, but it didn't matter, the damage was done.

Dad glared at me, then angrily tossed the ball aside as he stormed into the camper. The game was over. Nan stood there with a happy little smile on her face. I was incredulous! I wasn't even sure what had happened. I followed Dad into the camper where he was already engaged in a heated discussion with my mom about how I learned to speak such language. Of course, I had heard not only the word "dammit," but also a healthy string of much more colorful metaphors from Dad's lips on a daily—if not hourly—basis from as far back as I could remember. But apparently this was immaterial. The fact that my little sister had heard *me* say "dammit" was intolerable.

He told me he was ashamed of me for using such a "bad" word. Apparently, I should feel equally ashamed. I only felt betrayed. Dad stormed off into the woods for dramatic effect, and Nan stood there with a sweet, self-satisfied smile on her face. She had won. I stood there, Dadless, while Mom gathered Nancy into her arms and read her a story. This is so unfair, I thought. Since there was no physical way to get back at Nancy, I sat down and remembered a time when *she* was the one who was crying … .

The Giant
Roller-Coaster Ride

The year was 1960. I was only six years old. Usually we preferred camping, but this year Dad, Mom, baby Nancy, and I were staying at a motel in the little coastal town of Capitola near Santa Cruz. Mom was feeding Nan some tomato-smelling baby food and Dad took me outside to swim in the creek under the old railroad trestle.

I really loved this time with him as we laughed and played in the water. To spend time alone with him and have his sole attention like this was special. The water was warm, and redwood-filtered sunlight played patterns on the gently flowing water as we splashed around. River trout darted around our legs, and Dad told me about how he had swum and fished there as a kid with his brothers.

Eventually, Mom came by with Nan and disrupted our reverie. She spoke to Dad about "going to the Boardwalk."

He said, "Okay," and scooped me out of the water. I was indignant. We were having fun!

"Daddy, how come we have to go on a bored walk?" I asked. "I want to swim some more!"

My dad explained that the Boardwalk was a really fun place and that I would be happy and love it.

"I don't wanna go on a bored walk!" I said again, but my protests were ignored at this point. I soon found myself dragged back to the room, unceremoniously stripped of my swimsuit, and dressed in a white blouse, blue shorts, and sandals with my hair pulled back in a ponytail. Nan just slept on the bed like a slug, well-fed and happy, not giving a damn what anyone did.

A short drive brought us to the Santa Cruz Beach Boardwalk, where a spectacular array of rides competed for our attention, waves crashed onto a white sand beach, hawkers called out from brightly colored prize booths, and eateries of every kind glittered like jewels with colorful snow cones, salty pretzels, bright red candy apples, juicy pink hot dogs, and chocolate-covered bananas.

"Is this the bored walk place?" I asked my dad, incredulous.

"Yes, Rosanne. I told you it would be fun." Dad smiled.

WOW! I was mesmerized. This was an amazing place! I wanted to do everything at once.

I was still pretty small. I had never been on a big roller-coaster ride. I remember looking up at the Giant Dipper roller coaster—which had been built back in the 1920s—hearing it roar and clatter above us. It would click its way up, up, up, to an impossible height, perch for a few precarious seconds at the top, and then thunder downward like a tsunami. It was a terrifying, fearsome, monster ride painted bright red and white. It dominated the Boardwalk skyline, the iconic roller coaster of the West Coast.

"Let's take a ride, Rosanne!" I heard Dad's voice in my ear.

What? Me ride on that screaming, shuddering monster? I didn't know what to say. My thoughts froze as Dad took my hand and pulled me toward the looming entrance tunnel. My life was passing before my eyes in slow motion. Surely I must be way too young? Too small? Nope, I was tall for my age and passed the minimum height requirement, even though older, shorter, mean-faced kids who really WANTED to go on that ride could not get through the turnstile gate. Suckers!

We crossed the threshold to the entrance corridor. I could see bright lights flashing and hear voices screaming on the other side of the wall as the coaster trains roared off, and more screams in the far distance as the cars thundered up and down the tracks on their perilous journey.

Maybe the guy who loaded the trains with the people would notice how small I was and stop my dad from taking me on this death trip? Maybe some well-meaning mother somewhere would step in and pull me from the queue? No one stopped us. Oh please, somebody help me, I thought.

We stepped into the train car. A whistle tooted, and the locking bar came down with an authoritative crash, firmly imprisoning any would-be, last-minute deserters. Then a horn blasted and the train pitched forward into the tunnel. Total dizzying blackness, twisting left and right, and plummeting ever downward into darkness—surely we were on the ride to hell. How deep did this thing fall?

There was a huge lurch as we reached bottom, and a loud clacking as the train emerged into daylight. Then it began its slow and terrifying ascent upward. CLACKA CLACKA CLACKA CLACKA CLAAAAACK! As we climbed higher and higher, I was sure I could see the whole world! The entire beach and Boardwalk were suddenly miniaturized, the whole city of Santa Cruz was laid out below, cars moving in the streets were tiny specks, and I swear I could see the earth's curvature as I gazed, glassy-eyed, at the blue Pacific Ocean below us. This is what astronauts must see as they blast off from Earth, I thought.

Then there it was, right in front of us! The TOP! We teetered on the edge of the precipice. We seemed to hang in the air as time stopped there at the summit! And then we plunged, straight down. We were traveling much too fast. Nooooo, we would VAPORIZE!

We hit bottom, lurched upward, and with dizzying speed we ripped around the gigantic curve at the top, shearing left with enough centrifugal force to fling us across the universe. Unfortunately for me, I was on the outside of the seat and the full force of my dad's body mass crunched into me. OW!

It was then, in that briefest of instants, in that split second, that I understood the impact of Einstein's famous equation, $E=mc^2$. As I was smashed against the side of that car, hurtling through space and time at twice the speed of light, feeling the full force of mass, gravity, and momentum crushing against me, I understood what a thousand equations could never quite capture. Being pulled into a black hole would have been easier.

Then it was up and down a series of dizzying rises and falls and more incredibly sharp turns, followed by a screeching, clacking, and tumultuous roar back into the train house, where more people waited for their turn at terror. We were done. My brain was still back at that terrifying summit.

"Well, what did you think?" Dad asked.

"You smashed me, Dad!" I answered.

"Hmmm," he said as he appraised me. "You look alright to me. Let's go get some ice cream." And off we went to find Mom, who was trying to entertain little Nancy.

The Haunted Castle and Nan

Nancy was easily frightened. All my father had to do to discipline her was give her a stern look, and she would burst into tears. For my part, repeated episodes of corporal punishment did little to diminish my determination to remain fiercely independent. I was always in search of adventure, breaking boundaries, and wandering off in search of new thrills.

That day, while Dad and I were on the roller coaster, Mom got the idea of taking Nan into the Haunted Castle ride. I guess Dad and I had been gone awhile because Mom got tired of waiting for us and decided to take Nancy on this spooky ride. It involved boarding a two-seated, hearse-shaped cart that crashed through a dark door and then followed a twisting, turning tunnel track lined with spooky creatures that would jump out at you. There were loud noises, lit-up ghouls, ghosts flitting by, screaming faces flashing, and even unseen things that touched your head. At the end was a loud siren that pierced the air in the pitch darkness. I loved that ride. It still exists today and is extremely popular with people of all ages.

Now, Dad and I must have been at least a thousand feet away from Mom and Nancy at that point, but it didn't matter. Suddenly, all heads in the entire amusement park whipped around in response to the piercing scream coming from the back of the Haunted Castle—it was Nancy screaming at the top of her lungs! The Haunted Castle siren had succeeded with its mission; a terrified child was screaming her head off at an agonizing volume. We raced over to the ride and got there just in time to see Mom and Nan coming out of the ride in their little creepy car. Nan's head was tilted back, still screaming and crying. She looked so little and so afraid. Mom felt like an absolute failure for bringing her on the ride.

"Flora, what were you thinking?" Dad asked.

"Well, you took Rosanne on that huge roller coaster . . . " Her voice faded away as she gathered her crying toddler into her arms.

I never forgot this day, and neither did Nancy. We had both been singularly traumatized in the space of twenty minutes.

Me with Mom at the Santa Cruz Beach Boardwalk

Playing Cards and Slap-Down Hands

Back in the 1960s there were no portable TVs or DVD players. There were no little electronic devices except for handheld transistor radios. When we camped in our little trailer, my dad let us listen to our radios outside during the day, but at night we often played cards and board games. Monopoly and Candyland were popular favorites, but so were our playing cards. I loved Old Maid, Nan loved to play Go Fish, and Mom and Dad loved to play gin rummy. Gary played with his Tonka trucks.

Dad was a big risk-taker, and he would hold lots of cards in his hand. Mom was unpredictable. You could never quite tell what she was thinking, and she always played it coy with her sexy little voice. She was quite stunning with her wavy dark hair and liquid brown eyes. My dad was the head of the family, but my mom knew how to twist my dad around deftly in the palm of her hand. And she understood the feminine wiles of card playing very well.

"C'mon, Flora, you've been holding those cards forever," Dad would complain.

"I'm just thinking, Carroll," she would reply, staring into her hands.

"Well, make your choice and let's get on with it, for godsake! Is this gonna go on all night?" Silence. She would not be rushed. So Dad would make his move and draw a card, slapping down three queens to impress us all. Nan and I watched intently from the upper bunk. Gary ignored it all as he continued to make trucking sounds in the background. He was oblivious.

Mom would quietly draw a card and intently stare at it for five minutes, until Dad exploded again. "Put a card down, Flora!"

"Well, I just don't know, Honey," she would whine, whereupon Dad would slap down three of a kind, again trying to impress us all. We were nonplussed. We knew Mom too well.

Finally, when the tension had built to an unbearable level, Mom would draw her final card, and then it all seemed to happen at once, Slap! Slap! Slap! Slap! Slap! Slap! As she matched all of his cards and slammed down four aces, three kings, the missing ten, the missing queen, three jacks, two straights, and four deuces. This kind of hand happened every time. "Am I doing it right?" she would ask innocently, as my dad flew into a rage and stomped outside.

Nan and I almost fell out of our bunk laughing, and even Gary looked up from his place on the floor. Mom was a master, and she never broke character, except for a very slight smile at the corners of her beautiful lips. "Time for bed, kids," she would sweetly say.

"What about Dad?" we asked.

"Don't worry. He'll be back in a while. Let's make up the beds now."

Afterward she would put out cookies for the raging monster outside, knowing that when he came back, he would be mollified with the goodies on the table. She would stick her head out the door and call, "Carroll, Honey, it's bedtime." A grumble or two would sound from the far end of the campsite. We heard the screen door gently open and close as she tiptoed outside to find him. We heard muffled talking for a while. Eventually she coaxed him back inside with the promise of Oreo cookies. A few moments of crunch and munch was followed by tooth brushing, grumbling, and getting into bed. Then we all tried to fall asleep before Dad's thunderous snoring started.

Braving the Waves

We often went to beaches to swim. When we were small, my dad would take us in twos out into the waves. One kid on each arm. He was a strong swimmer, so waves weren't fearsome for him. He often dragged us out to the deeper water, where our feet reached desperately to touch the ocean floor.

Big, thundering, crashing waves would tumble toward us, with rough seas roiling all around. We would stand there, terrified of being knocked over, pulled under, and dragged off by a ferocious undertow, never to be seen again. The deep green water seemed bottomless, just waiting to swallow us. The waves would come, towering, charging, tumbling, and threatening to break us to bits. My dad would laugh out loud and lift his strong arms up into the air, swinging us high. As we hung on, the waves crashed around us. Whooossh! Wave after wave, and we were always lifted up high above the water.

We shouted in anticipation, daring the waves to come at us, because our dad would always protect us from harm and make us laugh. Dad stood his ground like a stone monument. Triumphant and victorious, we screamed with delight and defiantly challenged the next wave to attack.

This was a thrilling game! What a joy it was to face a deadly attacker and leap up away from its fearsome grasp, again and again, over and over! We laughed uproariously, looking up at Dad in amazement. How could anyone be so strong and mighty? We were in awe.

In many ways, Dad's mightiness gave us a strong sense of self-confidence. If he could lift us above the waves, we could learn to swim in them too. Years later, I would return to the beach with friends and fearlessly body surf waves in all kinds of weather.

But even a superhero needs his rest at some point, and eventually Dad would tire and ignore our passionate pleas to continue. He carried us back through the waves, one child clasped under each huge bear-like arm, and deposit us onto our beach towels.

There, Mom would be waiting with lunch. If we were in a sunny place like Santa Cruz, we would enjoy eating at the beach—happy, warm days having a nice beach picnic. We would enjoy our food and then wade back out into the water. But if we went to the ocean near our home in foggy Pacifica, things were different. There we were faced with freezing cold days at the beach.

Back then, before climate change warmed the skies in the San Francisco Bay Area, Pacifica was nearly always cold, wet, windy, foggy, and drizzly. It seemed to rain frigid droplets from all directions inside dense, cold, impenetrable fog. But nothing seemed to deter my mom from taking us to the beach. She loved the ocean. She was drawn to it. She would trundle us into the car: Nancy, Gary, and me.

Off we went to Sharp Park Beach in Pacifica where the wind whipped around, slapping our hair into hard wet strings, which then stabbed our eyeballs. Dark black sand polluted our drinks and covered our food with a crunchy gray crust. There was no escaping this. A sand-crusted bologna sandwich was not something to be enjoyed. Nevertheless, we were ordered to enjoy our picnic, and as my teeth crunched down on the gritty food my stomach churned in response UGH! It was awful.

This beach was nothing like the white, sandy beaches and soft, warm waters extolled in the popular rock songs of the time. I saw these beaches in Hollywood films, with stars like Sandra Dee, Frankie Avalon, and Annette Funicello, reclining in comfort on sunlit beach blankets. But the scene in front of me looked nothing like this. The harsh wind whistled in my ears, threatening to knock us all flat.

"Stop complaining," Mom said. "Now go and play in the water. You are at the beach, have fun!"

"It's too cold!" we complained, but this fell on deaf ears. In resignation, we slowly rose from our towels where we had been huddling in a shivering mass, desperately seeking body heat and survival from the merciless fog. We trudged across the gravelly black sand and slowly inched our toes into the icy waves. Ohhhh, it was SO COLD!

"Just jump in!" Mom shouted to us. Was this some sort of twisted sadism, we wondered? What had we done to deserve such cruelty?

We leapt into the freezing water and came up gasping. Windy gales of moisture-laden fog ripped past our ears as we splashed around in the opaque seas. Waves tumbled past and some knocked us down, rolling us over and over in the surf and covering our heads with sand. It filled our nostrils, our ears. Nancy whimpered and stayed near the edge of the water. We had to stay in for at least ten minutes or Mom sent us back in again.

If we were brave, we could get some cookies afterward, although they tasted like cardboard to our frozen lips after we came out. Mom bought boxes of vanilla wafers and these were tasteless. Our skin was blue, we were freezing to death, and we huddled beneath wet towels with sand in our hair.

"It wasn't so bad," Mom said. "You're lucky to be at the beach."

We longed for the comfort of home. Yet each of these times at the beach, whether in sunny Santa Cruz or foggy, cold Pacifica, taught me not to be afraid of nature, but instead to embrace it. Nature, as I learned, was something to be respected. Feared, yes, but enjoyed, no matter the weather. The whole world was out there and we were immersed in it. I'm thankful my parents taught us to brave the elements and rejoice in being outdoors.

Sleeper Wave!

I remember one fateful day in 1964, when we were at Thornton State Beach in Daly City, a few miles south of San Francisco. We were there with another family, and a sudden "sleeper" wave nearly killed us. I had heard stories about how rock fishermen were sometimes knocked down by big waves that picked them off rocks and carried them out to sea. I wasn't sure if these stories were tall tales or truth. But, after that day, I would never doubt the veracity of these tales again.

There were eight of us at the beach that day, six kids and two dads. No doubt the moms had demanded a break from all the kid-dom so they could relax and talk in peace. After all, the beach was a safe place to take the kids, right?

I remember that day with incredible clarity. We were all splashing and playing in the water. It was freezing cold as usual, but we were used to it, and had even learned to enjoy it over the years. I was ten and Nancy was five. The youngest in our group was a little boy from the other family, Michael, who was about three. Gary was at home for a nap that day.

We had been there for about an hour and the two dads were right there in the water playing with us. Suddenly, the water pulled rapidly away out to sea, and my dad shouted, "Get out of the water, now! Run! Rosanne, take your sister and run to the cliffs—DO IT NOW! RUN!!!" I grabbed my sister's hand and we all made a desperate race across the beach toward the steep hillside behind us.

Why wasn't Dad coming with us? How was I supposed to do this alone? I was terrified at the tone in his voice. Why did we have to run away from the shore? What terrible thing was happening? I felt abandoned, but I understood we were in danger and did what I was told. I ran with Nancy as fast as I could. Then I saw it coming, a huge cresting wave! It was enormous. It blotted out the horizon as it raced toward us with terrifying speed.

I looked back over my shoulder and saw everyone else running with us, except for my Dad. He was racing back to the beach to grab little Mike, who was sitting in the sand, looking placidly out to sea as swiftly impending death came cresting toward him. In split seconds, my father sprinted to little Mike, hoisted him onto his shoulders, and ran like hell toward us. We climbed way up the hillside, but I knew we were not going to escape the rushing water. Within seconds we were engulfed by a gigantic wave. We struggled and clawed upward, trying desperately to escape being pulled under. It was like a living monster was trying to devour us and suck us down into its dark and terrifying depths. [1]

The water crested at least halfway up the hillside, soaking our legs, and nearly dragging us back down with it. I held fast to Nan's hand and

---

1   This 'sleeper wave' was likely related to the Alaskan Earthquake and Tsunami of March 2, 1964. It was the largest U.S. earthquake ever recorded, at a magnitude of 9.2 in the Prince William Sound region of Alaska. The resulting tsunami spread all along the northern Pacific coast, killing at least 130 people.

watched as the other dad held onto three of his four children, looking on helplessly as my heroic father raced up the hill behind us with little Mike in his arms. They barely made it. I couldn't believe it; my dad was like a superhuman. I had never seen anyone move so fast. He saved that little boy's life.

Afterward, my mother questioned him about it: why hadn't he raced to save his own children? But I understood. Dad knew we would make it; he trusted me to get Nan to safety. He had a terrible choice to make. How could he leave that little boy to die? We were all shaking, shivering, terrified. But we had survived. I learned a frightening lesson: the ocean is always dangerously alive.

The Stolen Picnic Table

Mom and Dad often took us on picnics to nearby redwood parks, lakes, and beaches. Sometimes the picnics were big family gatherings with Italian grandparents and all the cousins, with huge foodie spreads—feasts, really. We would have Mom's delicious homemade potato salad, home-fried chicken, pickles, potato chips, sodas, chocolate torte, chocolate chip cookies, cakes, and pies. It was glorious food abundance.

Mostly, though, it was just our little family. With kids to dress and church to attend on Sundays, we rarely got our act together before two p.m. So, by the time we completed our drive and got to a favorite picnic spot, all the tables were taken. This happened every time, without fail.

"Dammit, Flora!" Dad scowled. "Why can't we get out of the house sooner? Now all the picnic tables are gone!" he raged.

"Carroll, Honey, I brought the big picnic blanket; we'll be fine," Mom said encouragingly, as she dragged out a sad-looking assemblage of ratty old blankets she had stitched together.

"I want to sit at a table," Dad grumbled, clearly disappointed to be relegated to the ground while his compatriots and their families sat upright, happy, and comfortable all around us. "And what's more, their stupid dogs pee all over the place! How will we keep them off our blanket?" Dad was really getting worked up now. "Look, there's one now—you see that stupid dog two tables over? It's peeing all over that other guy's blanket! Damn dogs! We need to sit up higher where we can keep track of who is doing what around here!" he roared. Clearly, my father was not the picnic blanket sort. "We're getting our own damned table, Flora; I swear it!" Dad scowled.

Eventually, Dad bought a brand-new, redwood picnic table with matching benches. He was so proud of that table. It stacked nicely into the back of his Chevy truck, too, which made him quite joyful. I thought it looked truly embarrassing and ridiculous, and I worried we might be accused of stealing it. But Dad was thrilled.

"Look, Flora!" he proudly announced. "Now we'll never have to sit on a stupid blanket again! See how this table fits in the truck? We can take it anywhere!"

Oh God, I thought. I was mortified.

The next weekend, Dad loaded his table up while Mom packed up our favorite picnic lunch. We were headed to San Gregorio State Beach, a lovely beach near Half Moon Bay, about thirty minutes south of San Francisco. There was a place on a bluff right above the ocean. Dad could hardly wait to grace this prime spot with his new acquisition.

On the highway heading down we got curious looks from other drivers as they doubtless wondered where we had stolen the picnic table from. They all stared and pointed as I shrank down in my seat.

We roared into the parking lot. Dad burst out of the truck triumphantly, while a turbulent dust cloud settled slowly around us. "Hah!" he chuckled, "our spot on the bluff is available. No one else took it!"

Well, of course no one else took it; there had been no table there, until now. "Help me get the picnic table out of the truck!" Dad said to Gary, who was maybe six years old and could barely carry a toy truck. But Gary obliged, and together they dragged it over gravel and up a steep hill to the coveted spot with the commanding ocean view. "Now we'll show those other smarmy bastards the right way to picnic!" Dad laughed heartily as he surveyed the picnic ground with a superior air.

All heads turned in our direction as the park patrons wondered where this madman had stolen that picnic table from. But there were also looks of jealousy in their eyes as if to say, "Why didn't we think of doing this?"

New arrivals spotted our table as they drove into the parking lot. How had they overlooked this spot in the past, they wondered? Had there always been a picnic table there? Why hadn't they noticed it before, and how long would they have to wait until they could use it? Why, it was in a prime spot!

Dad looked around proudly as Mom spread the tablecloth and laid out our lunch. "Look at that view!" Dad exclaimed. "You can see the waves crashing! Feel the sea spray! No dogs running around up here! No waiting for another family to leave; this is ours! All ours!" He was so jubilant. And it was a great spot, perched on a bluff above the ocean.

San Gregorio Beach is a joy with a wide, sandy beach and rock caves to explore. It's often sunny there and the ocean is clear and blue. Pine and redwood forest surrounds the park, with gentle farm pastures and coastal marshes emptying into the sea.

I helped Mom lay out the lunch, but I felt the hot burn of accusing stares from our fellow picnickers. I felt like a total jackass. What kind of bozos bring their own table to a crowded picnic area, anyway?

As we sat down to eat, I could see the new arrivals queuing up to use our table, just waiting for us to finish and leave so they could have the spot with the best view. "Dad, I feel really self-conscious," I whined, worrying that we might be arrested for illegal picnicking.

"Quiet, Rosanne! We have every right to be here. This is our picnic table. Just enjoy the great view." But still, I felt like we were in the center of a goldfish bowl as I tried to eat my sandwich. Everyone was staring at us, even the dogs.

Me and Dad at San Gregorio State Beach. Nancy and Gary in the background on right

Eventually, we finished our meal and began packing up the food so we could go play on the beach. But now we faced a problem: how would we keep others away from the table? "Just leave the tablecloth on, Flora," Dad said. But other would-be diners were already quickening their steps uphill, frantically trying to outpace each other, running with picnic baskets under their arms and dogs barking excitedly at their sides, racing to be the first to claim our table.

"Hey, buddy, don't hog the table!" one particularly fierce-looking man with a storm cloud of about ten kids said. "You've had your lunch, and now you wanna keep the table to yourself while you go off to the beach? Give it up, you asshole!" The man's wife looked even scarier than him, and bigger too. She had a steamroller quality about her.

"It's our table!" Dad shouted.

"This is a public beach, jerk!" the man hollered back. "You can't just hog a table all to yourself!"

Uh-oh, I thought. This could get ugly fast. Whereupon Dad ripped the tablecloth off, crumpled it up and threw it into our picnic basket in a gesture of all-out war. He muttered a stream of obscenities. Then he proceeded to load *his* picnic table onto *his* truck, benches and all.

"HEY!" the other man shouted, "You can't steal public property! Put that table back right now! We've been waiting to use it!

"Well, you can wait until hell freezes over!" Dad shouted back.

"Honey, let's just go now," my poor Mom said, as a large crowd began to gather.

"But, Flora, I wanted to play on the beach with the kids," Dad cried. He had brought a big, colorful beach ball for us to play with, but he knew we couldn't just walk away from that picnic table now. He had created his own problem by bringing it here. Someone would steal it, whether it was stacked in the truck or not. He hadn't considered this possibility when he bought the table. Did we really have to leave now, right when he was ready to have fun on the beach? It just wasn't fair! Dammit!

Then a park ranger showed up. He looked at the little knot of people gathered around the picnic table loaded onto a truck. Clearly, he was puzzled. Had a crime been committed? He wasn't quite sure. The picnic table in the truck did not have the look of a state park table, but where had it come from?

"Flora, get the kids in the truck NOW!" Dad hollered. "We'll go someplace else!"

Hurriedly, we gathered up the remnants of our lunch and jumped into the vehicle as Dad gunned the accelerator. We charged out of the parking lot, creating a huge dust cloud as the confused park ranger stood there completely stunned and wondering if he should give chase. In my later years as a park ranger, I would look back on this moment and feel sorry for that poor fellow, perplexed as to what to do.

Dad floored the gas pedal as the secondary and tertiary accelerators of his V-8 engine roared to life, lifting us off the pavement and blasting us northward up Highway 1, threatening to break the sound barrier.

The Dreaded Family Camp

One summer in 1966, my parents got the idea of going to one of those family-themed camps where everything is provided for you. The place was somewhere north of San Francisco in the Clear Lake area. It was like the family camp in the movie *Dirty Dancing,* but much lower class. Instead of a nice, clean, upscale cottage with full bath, kitchen, cozy furniture, and fancy rugs like in the movie, we were assigned to a dark, smelly tent cabin with dirt floors and no toilet. It had wooden platforms for sleeping bags. The walls were greasy from indoor cooking. It was disgusting.

There was a kid's playground, a central gazebo, a small camp store, and a laundromat. A mess hall dominated the center of the establishment. The food was terrible. They served ghastly things like chipped beef in mystery white goo sauce, and greasy-looking noodles with some unknown meat that was supposedly chicken. Breakfast was corn flakes with rehydrated powdered milk. Double ugh!

The camp leaders organized games and provided music and folk dancing in the gazebo. I hated that place. It was crowded and hot, with tons of bugs, and there was dirt everywhere. There were too many people. I wanted to have a real camping experience, not stay in this fake camping venue.

There were play activities. I was a really fast runner and competed in a game which I easily won. For my victory I was given a free coupon to get a snack at the camp store. I really loved barbecue potato chips and I ran to the shabby little camp store to get them. On the way there, I tripped over a tree root and skinned my knee. Undaunted, I nursed my wound and hobbled into the store. It was a camp building with wooden walls, an open-beam ceiling, and a very limited selection of groceries. Dusty commodities sat morosely on sagging shelves. Behind the counter stood a very bored male employee.

"Hey, where are the candy bars?" I asked.

"Ain't got none," was the reply. Sheesh, this place sucks, I thought.

I bought my cherished barbecue chips and stuffed them into my mouth, and then ran to our tent cabin to get a Band-Aid. Mom looked at my knee and asked what happened. I told her about the fall and she said, "Serves you right for running."

I thought this was a bit harsh, but Nan thought it was pretty funny. She was clearly bored and I had provided a bit of fun entertainment, running in with my skinned knee. I felt very hurt and annoyed. Here I had won a race and been rewarded with free barbecue chips, and now I was the subject of ridicule. Not fair! I thought.

Wow, I thought, life is rough. I crunched the remainder of my chips pensively. "How long do we have to stay here?" I asked.

"She's right, Flora, I don't like this place either," Dad said. "I know you thought it would be nice, but the kids all seem to hate it here."

"Gary likes it," Mom said.

"Well of course he does, Honey. The cafeteria is all you can eat!"

Gary looked up from the bench where he was playing with his trucks and smiled. He could be happy anywhere, I thought to myself. In a way, I envied him.

Drowning, Anyone?

Later that same summer, Mom and Dad thought it might be nice for me to go with my aunt and uncle and their four kids to Clear Lake. I could spend several days with them and then the whole family would get together on the weekend. I thought this sounded fun; we were going to stay in a waterfront house and could go swimming every day.

My uncle Sal picked me up and escorted me to their car full of kids. There were four cousins about my age to hang out with. We had all played together since we were babies and got along well.

We set out from the San Francisco Bay Area heading north along Highway 101, and then east on Highway 20 toward Clear Lake. Highway 20 winds through the California Coastal Range and is a very tortuous route. Somewhere along the way, I got carsick. I told my uncle I felt ill, but he wouldn't stop the car. I said I was going to vomit, but still he would not stop. I couldn't believe it. I felt horribly queasy and knew I could not hold it back any longer.

"I'm going to throw up!" I shouted.

"Open the window and stick your head out," I was told.

Good grief! Why wouldn't he stop? I had no choice but to vomit out the window and all over the car. My cousins all found this very amusing and laughed out loud. What was so funny, I wondered? I had made a terrible mess and I felt horrified.

"She threw up all over the car, Daddy!" they all chorused happily, intrigued that I had committed such a gross act.

"We'll rinse it off when we get there," my uncle answered. I was mortified.

This ill wind should have portended what was to come.

That weekend my mom, dad, siblings, and grandparents joined us. All of us kids were swimming in the lake with tire inner tubes (the equivalent of plastic floaties in today's world). I liked to drop down and touch the lake bottom with my feet every so often because I didn't want to drift off into deep water. I didn't really know how to swim yet, only how to float on my stomach. Our parents were on shore and they were not really watching us that closely. I guess they thought that since we had the floatation tubes, we were alright.

At one point, I slid down through my inner tube to touch bottom—except there was no bottom. I had floated into deeper water! I tried to scramble back into my inner tube but it had already floated away from me. I panicked. Suddenly I realized I could die. I was having a near-death experience as thoughts raced rapidly through my brain. The water rushed around me, enveloping me like a darkening cloak. I was sinking. I was going to drown!

Somehow, in my desperate panic, I remembered my beginner's swimming lessons. I hadn't learned to swim, but I had practiced floating on my stomach many times. I quickly spread my arms and legs out and slowly drifted back toward shore. After a moment I was back in the shallow water again, and I was able to kick toward the beach.

I could hear my idiotic cousins laughing at me in the background. "What were you doing, Rosanne? You looked so funny the way you had your arms and legs sticking out!" they taunted.

I concluded that they were all idiots as I ran onto shore and told my parents what happened. But no one would listen to me. They were too engaged in their adult conversations. I couldn't believe it; I had nearly lost my life, and no one seemed to notice, or care. They all thought I was making up stories! Unbelievable!

Afterward, I swore to myself that when I had kids, I would never let them into the water without a life jacket. Parents often get distracted when their children are in the water when, in truth, they should never take their eyes off them for a second.

This near-fatal experience taught me to become a good swimmer when I grew older. In later years, as a park ranger at places like Folsom Lake and Lake Oroville in California, I responded to drownings where family members had taken their attention away from swimmers for "only a minute" and lost their loved ones. These moments still seem painfully real to me, many years later.

Tent Trailer Woes

"Hey, Flora, why don't we try using a tent trailer for this year's camping trip? I've been looking at these things in rental ads, and they seem to have a lot more room inside than a metal trailer," Dad marveled to my mom one day.

"But Honey, aren't those things difficult to use? Why not just rent a regular trailer like we've done before?" Mom wondered out loud.

"Flora, you just crank them open and drop the door into place. It will be easy! We'll have more room inside, because the sides expand outward, creating twice the space. Plus, we'll have nice, clean air inside like being in a tent, but with all the modern conveniences. It will be great!"

Mom looked concerned. She didn't like the idea at all. The rest of us stared suspiciously at the pictorial illustration showing a happy family camping inside one of those things. Undeterred by our lack of enthusiasm, Dad rented one for our trip to the Santa Cruz coast that spring. There was even an option to buy it later if we liked it.

Nowadays, a tent trailer is a great option for family camping with easy-to-use pop-outs and all kinds of modern conveniences. They are easy to set up and take down again. But back in the late 1960s, tent trailers were clunky monsters made out of heavy canvas with primitive hand-crank systems for opening and closing. I think my dad must have rented one of the earliest versions known to mid-twentieth-century Homo sapiens.

The week for our trip arrived in late April. Dad proudly went to pick up the tent trailer and tow it home. He set it up in the driveway outside so we could load it up the day before the trip.

"It smells bad!" Nancy sniffed. She scowled and backed away from it.

She was right, it *did* stink—odors of Unknown Origin wafted out from the dark interior. Who had rented this thing before us? Where had they taken it? What on earth had they done to it? These questions would remain unanswered, locked deep within the canvas depths.

"Where did you rent this thing from, Dad?" I asked.

"Never mind that," Dad said. "Look at all the space in here! We'll have lots more sleeping room now. See, you just crank this section open and—yeeoouch!" he hollered as the cranking mechanism caught on his shirt sleeve, taking some arm skin along with it. This should have served as a clear warning that a canvas monster in the guise of a trailer was perhaps not the best camping idea. But Dad was undeterred. With his now-bleeding arm, he reattached the metal lever and again began cranking the top upward and the sides outward. It looked like some prehistoric dinosaur unfurling its massive wings. Gradually, with much creaking and clanking, the top lifted and the sides expanded open.

"There!" Dad exclaimed triumphantly as he successfully locked the sides into place. "Kids, go ahead and hop onto those beds and see what you think."

We peered inside reluctantly, afraid that perhaps the entire thing might collapse and swallow us like some monster devouring its prey. I climbed inside and rolled onto one of the beds. It *was* a lot roomier than the rigs we'd camped in before. Maybe it would be alright. "Can I have this bunk?" I asked.

"You can share it with Nancy or Gary, take your pick," Mom replied. I wondered if I would ever have my own bed on any trip. At least Nancy didn't fart. Gary's farts were legendary.

The next day we were on our way, and the trailer clanked along behind us. "It's so much easier to haul than a regular trailer, so much lighter," Dad told Mom as we rolled down Highway 1.

When we got to the park, Dad expertly backed into the campsite. Then he cranked open the top and tried to unfurl the sides. But the crank mechanism jammed. "Dammit!" Dad cried. "This worked at home, now what the heck is wrong?" He rummaged around in his toolbox and pulled out a wrench. But no matter what he did, the thing was jammed. He tried using a hammer and banged against the wrench, hoping to force the cantankerous mechanism to dislodge. Still no luck.

Great, we were two hours from home and now our trailer was jammed shut. Repeated obscenities directed at the mechanism bore no fruit. Finally, Mom had an idea.

"Should we try some oil?" she offered.

"That's it!" Dad shouted. He opened up the trunk of our car and dug out an old can of WD-40. Taking this inside, he liberally sprayed down the recalcitrant crank system.

"Honey, you're getting that spray everywhere," Mom said.

"Quiet, Flora, I think this is going to work!" In the next instant, the creaking mechanism was released and the wrench went flying through the air, nearly whacking him on the head. Success! Dad triumphantly opened the sides and we were all set.

We had a great deal of fun for the next few days playing on the beach, having picnics in our camp, and shopping in the little villages in the area. It was a great time to be alive and we really enjoyed our time together as a family. But this was April, not summer. And in April, it often rained. On the fourth day of our trip, it started to drizzle. Then more drops fell, and by that afternoon, it began to rain in earnest. We clambered inside our rig to seek shelter. Now it became apparent why more families were not camping in tent trailers. Water began cascading down the outsides.

"Maybe we should go stay at a motel?' Mom suggested.

"No, Flora, we came here to camp," Dad insisted. "It will blow over and we'll be fine."

Water was seeping inside through the seams in the canvas. I watched in fascination as it dripped down onto the bunks—and onto our sleeping bags. "Get those bags off the bunks!" Dad ordered, whereupon we dragged them onto the floor.

"Kids, sit down at the table until this storm passes," Mom said. "Eat some snacks—here are some cookies." Cookies were Mom's solution to most crises. We munched pensively as we waited for the storm to pass. By now the bunks were soaked from all the rainwater coming in. They made a squishy noise when we touched them.

"I thought these tent trailers were supposed to be waterproof," Dad said apologetically. "But wasn't it great sleeping in here the last three nights? It felt like being outdoors, right kids?"

"Sure, Dad," I said. In a way, he was right. It was nice to sleep in the tent trailer because you could hear the sounds of the night: frogs croaking, crickets chirping, owls hooting, the distant call of coyotes off in the hills. But a wet bed wasn't supposed to be part of the experience. At least, I didn't think so. I wondered how prehistoric people had dealt with rainstorms. How did they manage to keep the water out of bark houses? They must have plugged the openings with a lot of tree limbs and moss. They were probably a lot smarter than us, I mused.

After about an hour the storm abated. Dad wiped down the tent so it would dry quickly. "Let's go down to the beach," Mom said.

Waves were crashing way up onto the sand. Big breakers roared up onto the beach and then sucked back down into the ocean. It was exhilarating. Big storms often brought beach treasure, and I searched around for flotsam. Dad found a colorful float and I found a soggy but bright travel pennant. Back then, families often bought little pennant flags to "capture" the places they visited, and then displayed these on their walls at home as travel trophies. This one was bright red, orange, blue, and yellow. It had drawings of the San Francisco skyline on it. It must have flown out of a passing car or escaped from a previous encampment.

"Good find, Rose!" Dad laughed. "We'll hang it up in our camp along with this float I got." Gary found a paddle-shaped board and began whacking pebbles with it, and Nan looked for shells. Everyone seemed happy, in spite of all our stuff getting wet. It really didn't matter if we had a fancy rig, we were having fun together.

Later on we went back to camp and dried all the stuff out. Dad hung the sleeping bags from nearby tree branches while Mom aired out the trailer. Sunlight filtered down through the cedar trees, making leaf shadow patterns across the forest floor. A wonderful fresh scent of evergreen permeated the air.

Mom went inside the trailer to make salami sandwiches, her favorite. Maybe there would be potato chips too? We rarely got those except on special outings. Sometimes Mom would buy the box with the different kinds of chips inside: corn chips, barbecue chips, regular chips, and curly cheese chips. We argued over who got what. Arguing was half the fun. Then came bargaining and trades.

We sat at the picnic table and got damp butts from the wet benches, but this was preferable to being inside the wet trailer.

Little brown chipmunks with black and white stripes scampered out of the bushes looking for handouts. "Don't feed them!" Dad warned, as they greedily edged forward.

"They look so cute," Mom said, as I surreptitiously tossed a crumb toward them. This was a strategic error. Suddenly there were six of them—then a dozen—all scooting toward our table and getting underfoot.

"Geeeyahh!" Dad shouted and they all ran away. "Now they won't leave us alone!" They were persistent, alright. It didn't take long before they crept back out and surrounded us again. We quickly finished eating and put the food away.

"I'm going to take a nap," Dad announced. He had finished his lunch and decided there had been enough excitement for one day.

When the going gets tough, the tough take a nap, I thought. Dad brought out his folding canvas recliner, laid down, and soon began snoring. It always amazed me how he could sleep anywhere, even sitting up. I envied him this ability.

Mom and Nan were reading books at the picnic table. "C'mon, Gary," I said, "let's go for a walk." We followed a sunlit creek and watched fish darting back and forth in deep pools.

"I wanna catch them," Gary said.

"Don't lean so far forward, Gary, you could fall in."

"Okay," he said, and jumped into the water up to his knees.

"Oh no! Mom is gonna kill us! Gary, your shoes are soaking wet!" Fortunately, he had shorts on or he would have been sopping wet. He was wearing high-top tennis shoes. And I was the one who would get in trouble for leading him to the creek. "We'd better head back and get some dry shoes on your feet before you catch cold. Come on, Gar-Bear, let's go." I took his little hand and pulled him out of the water. Now there would be wet tennis shoes to go with the wet tent trailer.

"I wanna see those fish!" he insisted. "Dad will come back with you later," I said, and gently pulled him away.

"Rosanne, what were you thinking letting him get in the water like that?" Mom scolded me.

"Sorry," I said sheepishly. This big sister stuff wasn't easy. I could see the chipmunks laughing at me from the bushes.

Years later, this mishap gave me a great idea for a ranger walk. I thought about how park visitors might like walking upstream with their tennis shoes on, learning all about river ecology. It was a popular activity, and the visitors who went on it wondered how I'd come up with the idea. I had my little brother to thank for this.

Walking in the Woods and the Wrath of Dad

In the years that followed, we made many trips back to the Big Sur coast. I loved to walk down the different trails in the park, breathing in the soul-calming scent of the redwoods. The coastal fog would crest and settle onto the ridges of the high granite mountains, but it never came down into the little protected valley where we camped.

Big Sur is a spectacular part of the coast and, at that point in time, this beautiful California state park hadn't really been discovered. Later, the early 1970s attracted a hippie movement into the entire region, and this park was never the same afterward. It had been discovered. The 1969 Summer of Love brought thousands to San Francisco, and eventually south to the redwood coastline of Big Sur.

But for now, on this spring day in 1968, it was tranquil and lovely. Lots of little families like ours came to camp here. Most had tiny little trailers like ours, or they set up big canvas tents. Motorhomes hadn't really been invented yet, and so evenings were quiet, peaceful, and free of generator noise. There were just happy campers during the day and glowing campfires in the evening. Little tendrils of smoke and soft voices drifted up through the gentle foliage of trees.

One afternoon Mom, Nancy, and I decided to take a walk through the campground toward the river gorge at the back of the park. I was fiercely independent and always walked way out in front. They were walking and talking so slowly! What on earth did they always talk about? Nancy was Mom's baby, her beloved little one. They were often inseparable. I didn't care. I had no interest in lagging along at Mom's side. I longed to journey out into the world alone and find new adventures.

Nancy had always been quieter, a shy, sweet girl who preferred to lie on her bed and read a book rather than go outside and experience the outdoors. I would often come indoors after playing with friends, and find her there, barely moving from where she had been that morning. Mom loved books too and read every chance she got.

"Why don't you come outside and play, Nancy?" I would ask her. "You're missing everything just lying there."

She would roll over and look at me like I was an alien intruding on her peaceful expanse. "Go away," she'd say.

I would sigh and leave her to her reveries, sad that she didn't want to join me outside. She was my baby sister and I loved taking her places, when she decided to come with me. But it could be tough to pry her loose from her books.

I was a young teenager and I loved to make new friends, especially boys. I would walk the campground and talk to people in the different campsites. It was fun, and I got to meet people from all over the world.

My father didn't like me talking to strangers, especially guys, so he got really angry with me at one point. I guess I'd been gone too much, too often, or too long.

Dad was an overprotective father. He had spent several years working as a volunteer law enforcement officer for the Pacifica Police Department, and he had seen what can happen to unsupervised young girls. He constantly tried to scare me, by telling me stories of teen pregnancies and the dangers of drugs. I listened and heeded his advice—most of the time. But I also longed for my freedom.

I couldn't do anything without Dad learning about it. He showed my photograph to everyone in our hometown. I couldn't buy a pack of cigarettes from a vending machine without the store owner calling my father. Once, I tried to sneak out of a movie theater and get in a car with some boys. Suddenly there was my father, waiting for me in a police car because the theater manager had seen me with the young men and called him! It was suffocating. I felt like Dad was in my way of growing up and I resented this. How was I supposed to meet anyone or go anywhere if I was constantly being dogged all the time? I wanted liberation and freedom from what I perceived as a growing tyranny over my precious independence.

When I came back from that innocent walk in the Big Sur campground on that fateful afternoon, Dad accused me of "trolling for men," even though I wasn't. I had simply been walking in the sunlight and talking to other campers. I couldn't believe he would think I was being immoral. I got so mad at him; I ran off. I was gone for hours. I just ran and ran until I was exhausted. I climbed all the way up the steep mountainside, until I finally collided with Highway 1.

Highway 1, the Pacific Coast Highway! The one in all the movies about California, surfers, the Beach Boys, television shows about motorcycle loners like *Then Came Bronson*, and everything wild and vagabond. It was beautiful, spectacular, adventurous, and glamorous. And here it was, shimmering right before me, beckoning me to escape. I reached down to touch it. I could feel it vibrating with energy.

I seriously thought about hitchhiking down the coast. I could finally be free and independent! I would show Dad, I thought. I could do what I wanted when I wanted, wear what I pleased, smoke and drink and learn about what it felt like to get high. My father had always put the fear of God into me over the idea of taking drugs, so I was a real drug virgin. And a real virgin in every way. An innocent little fool.

The whole world lay before me with the promise of Highway 1. I could head south to Malibu and hang out on beautiful, white sand beaches there. I could swim in a warm, gentle ocean. I knew I could find people to buy things for me, and I would easily survive just fine. Or I could head north to Oregon or Washington where the forest marched straight down to the sea. I could live in a little sea shack on a beach and wake to the sounds of the waves every morning.

But these happy thoughts of freedom were eclipsed by the realization of how much Dad and Mom cared about me, and of how worried my dad probably was feeling. Would my siblings even care if I were gone? I wondered.

I still thought hard about leaving, though. The thought of total freedom was intoxicating, and all I had to do was put my thumb out. I knew I could get a ride in sixty seconds or less. I also knew I could end up dead. In the years to come, there would be many serial killers in California picking up young women just like me. Many of those women ended up dead in ways too awful to imagine. Was it worth it? I wondered.

I turned around and slowly trudged back to camp. As I walked up to our campsite, my dad was sitting outside with his head in his hands. He was crying. I felt terrible, like the worst kid in the world for making him feel this way. I was guilty, like a traitor, for causing him grief. I knew he hadn't really meant what he said; he was just trying to protect me. He looked up and saw me. He looked so surprised and relieved. He was at a loss for words, for the right thing to say. Then suddenly he blurted out, "Everything I do is for you kids and your mother!" And then, sensing his own embarrassment, he stormed inside the trailer to the comforting solace of Mom.

"It's alright, Carroll, Honey," I heard her tell him. I could hear low and muffled voices for a long time in there. Later on, Dad came outside and just sat quietly by the campfire. We didn't talk, just sat quietly together.

And that was the end of that. Neither of us ever spoke of that time again. From that day forward, anytime we had a disagreement, we talked about it. There would be no more running away.

Hey Man,
Your Boots Are Smokin!

The following year in 1969, we were at Big Sur Campground, and I had made friends with two guys in a nearby site. The younger one, who was actually kind of an idiot, came by after dinner to talk to me. By now my Dad was getting used to the fact that guys were going to show up around me, regardless of whether he liked the idea or not. He made a show of being the *cool* dad and even offered the visiting dope a shot of his favorite whiskey. The guy gulped it down in a half second and looked around for more. Dad refilled the glass and tried to engage the guy in conversation, but no intelligent exchange ensued.

My father decided to call it a night and, after tucking the whiskey bottle under his arm, he told me not to stay up past eleven p.m. "I'll be right on the other side of this trailer door, Rosanne, so mind the time. Watch yourself, and don't put your feet too close to that fire," he directed in a loud voice, as he stomped off to bed.

We had a campfire going in one of those big concrete campsite grills. It was a little bit chilly out, so I stretched out my legs and extended my boot tips toward the edge of the fire to warm up my feet. I had my very trendy army surplus jacket on to keep the rest of me warm.

The guy and I talked about all kinds of stuff: the places we'd been, where we hoped to go, how much beer you could drink before falling down drunk, who our favorite rock stars were—all the big questions in life. It was an easy conversation, and we soon lost track of time.

"Maybe you shouldn't get your feet too close to that fire," the guy said at one point, as a little wisp of smoke started to spiral off the bottom of my boots.

But I shrugged it off, with a "Who cares?" We went on talking.

We started discussing other stuff, like who we had dated, what we wanted to do someday, where we would travel if we had cars of our own, and—what was that smoky smell of burning rubber, and where was it coming from?

A couple of raccoons came out of the shadows, hoping for a handout, but we shooed them away. By now I had wised up to their antics and recognized them for the shamefaced, gluttonous little opportunists they were. "Go away, you little beasts! Why are you here anyway?" I shouted at them.

"What's going on out there?" my dad hollered from inside the trailer.

"Nothing, Dad!" I called back. My guy friend and I snickered at this intrusion on our privacy.

Then I heard my little brother's voice say, "What are they doing out there, Dad? Are they kissing or something?"

"Quiet, Gary, go to sleep," my dad snorted.

"Man, your family is really nervous," the guy said.

"Yeah, I know," I told him. "But don't worry, they'll go to sleep soon."

By now one of the more daring members of the raccoon gang had edged its way up to the fire pit. "Scat!" I hissed, and the thing growled at me as it retreated.

"Man, those creatures are scary," the guy said as he slid closer to me in a ploy to get more familiar.

"Yeah, they're always looking for food, but usually not at this hour," I said, clearly puzzled as to why so many of them had appeared all of a sudden. I edged away from the guy, not really liking where this was going.

"Hey man, your boots are smokin!" the guy shouted.

"Damn!" I wailed, as I suddenly understood why the raccoons had gathered for the barbecue—and I knew in an instant what a hot foot felt like. As I struggled to get my boots off before my feet burned, I realized I should have listened to my father. Again.

I said goodnight to the guy and trudged inside our trailer for the night, leaving my smoking boots at the door, along with my wounded pride. The campfire coals, sated from my sacrificial offering, mockingly gleamed back at me.

The next morning, I got a stern lecture from Dad about fire safety. "You were supposed to douse the flames afterward," he admonished. "And how in the heck did you manage to melt your boots? Do you not think at all?" he asked in exasperation. I had nothing intelligent to say. "And that guy was an idiot!" he said. Again, I had nothing intelligent to say. "Go help your mother with breakfast," he said, shaking his head in total frustration at my complete abdication of common sense.

I'd learned an important lesson firsthand: the best way to prevent forest fires is by not setting your own feet on fire.

Let's Go Out in a Boat with Those Strangers

Dad got a better trucking job and eventually got more time off. This meant we were able to go on more trips. Later that year we went camping on the Oregon coast. I was walking along the shore of a bay in a coastal park and had met two older guys. They said they had a cabin cruiser boat anchored offshore. Nancy was with me. She was only ten and I was fifteen.

"Wanna go out to our boat this evening?" one of the guys said. "You can meet us on shore at dusk and we can row you out there." They said this was about a quarter mile offshore. "We'll have food and drinks for everyone."

Like a total imbecile, I thought this sounded fun. "Can I bring my sister?" I stupidly asked.

"Sure, she's welcome," the lecherous bastards replied.

"Hey Nancy, you wanna go out with those guys and see their boat this evening?" I asked her.

Now my little sister was no dope, even at ten years. She eyed me suspiciously. "I think we should ask Mom and Dad," she intoned.

"Don't be silly, Nan. Dad will say no. Those guys invited us and they have drinks and appetizers. I want to go see their boat. It will be fun. They said they can take us on a cruise around the harbor. We can just say we are going for a walk later, and go see their boat instead," I idiotically concluded.

"Okay," Nan said, knowing it was pointless to argue. She may have been five years younger but, somehow, she was five years smarter.

"We'll be back later," I told the two waiting men.

"We'll be here," they grinned.

A couple hours went by and dusk approached. I went to retrieve Nancy. "Mom, we're going for a walk by the harbor. Nan, c'mon!" I called in through the screen door of the camper. But instead of being joined by my traitorous sister I got my dad, who stormed outside and grabbed my hand, dragging me down the path and out of earshot of Mom and family.

"Just what the hell were you thinking, Rosanne?" he scolded me. "It's bad enough you would put yourself in a dangerous situation, but to drag your little sister along too? Are you really that stupid?" He was really playing the personal guilt card. "Do you honestly think those men were going to serve you drinks and appetizers? Or do you think that maybe you and your sister would have been on the menu?"

"Dad, we only wanted to see their boat," I said, as I stared dumbly ahead.

"Yup, you would've seen it, alright, but not in the way you think. How can you be so clueless? Just when I think maybe you've acquired some basic sense, you come up with a lunatic idea like this. Don't you give a damn about your life? Your sister's life? Just what the hell do you suppose would have happened out there? A dockside, candlelight supper? They would have taken off with you, and they would have hauled you far away too! And then what do you suppose would've happened? And whatever happened, it would not have been just to you, but to your little sister too! You're a fool if you think otherwise!"

Now I had heard countless talks from my dad about personal safety, the dangers of drug use, why men are dangerous, teen pregnancy, and more—over and over. But I still went out and did dumb stuff, just like any teenager would.

But my dad really hit home when he painted a vivid picture of what could have happened if Nan had not told him about my brilliant plan. Years later, I watched a movie called *Sudden Impact* about a young girl who brings her little sister to a party, and both are brutally gang-raped. The little sister is never the same afterward, and the older sister is left with lifelong guilt, punctuated with a bloody quest for revenge.

In that moment, years before I'd ever heard of that film, I understood what my dad was saying. And I realized that what he was describing could have actually happened to us. We could have both ended up dead. And who would have known? Who would have heard our cries for help out there on the open water? I was shocked at my own shortsightedness.

"You just stand here and think about that for a while!" Dad said, as he stormed off.

I never forgot that moment. I can clearly recall it now, fifty years later. What the hell was I thinking? I wondered. Was I so anxious for adventure that I routinely thrust all thought of personal safety aside? How could I have put us both at risk? It was unthinkable.

"I told Dad what you said!" Nan triumphantly announced when I came in for dinner.

"Yes, you did," I quietly responded.

"You're in trouble!" she happily informed me.

"No, but we could have been," I said. My sister just stared at me, unsure of what was going on.

"Eat your dinner, Nancy," Mom said, while Dad glared at me.

I grew up a great deal that night.

Years later, when I was a park ranger, I was involved in many missing person searches for children and adults. Some of these searches had begun just like this situation, where one or more young women had gone off with strangers like these men. Many of these unfortunate young women came back traumatized, injured, assaulted, or worse. Looking back, I'm glad my sister spoke to my Dad and stopped us from such a potentially perilous journey.

Blue Poop

We spent many summers camping along the Oregon and Washington coast in little family trailers with no toilet, always choosing campsites right next to public restrooms. I hated this, because it meant being next to a noisy area with the sound of turbocharged toilets flushing, loud voices, showers running, and blinding bright lights on all night.

It was hard to relax and enjoy the peace of nature with the sound of jet propulsion toilets flushing every five minutes in the nearby restrooms. Why couldn't we choose a site further away? There were some lovely ones right across the road overlooking the creek. Or perhaps one under the towering redwood trees, bathed in evergreen shadows? But, no, Nan still needed the restroom several times a night. I could never understand this. Why couldn't she just go once and sleep through the night instead of waking my poor mom, and making her trudge through the campsite to the restroom? Gary just peed in the campsite, so Dad got off easy. It wasn't fair.

Then one year, my Dad worked several extra jobs to save up money and proudly rented a motorhome. It had a toilet and shower combination, full kitchen, spacious sleeping accommodations (I still had to share a bunk with Nan), and all the amenities.

He proudly rolled it home on the eve of our departure with a beaming smile on his happy face. "This year we're camping in style with our own bathroom. No more Mom having to get up at night with Nancy—Nan, here you are, your own private toilet!"

Nancy looked suspicious. Why would Dad do this awful thing? I was worried too, I had seen these obnoxious, noisy rigs in campgrounds and thought they were abominations. The noise from motorhome generators destroyed the peace of the forest.

But there it was, a full-blown, five-alarm, motorhome adventure lurking right in front of our house.

Of course, having your own toilet and shower meant having to dispose of your own sewage. No more dumping gray water onto the ground. Even this was against the law, but Dad had always stuck a bucket under the trailer for appearance's sake, but in truth we obnoxiously dumped gray water all over the campsite like everyone else in those days. However, the motorhome was supposedly a *self-contained*, sealed system. Of course, those motorhome designers did not know my father.

Now there was noxious black water to dispose of, and this loathsome task was accommodated in campgrounds, which provided a sewage disposal station. But most campgrounds did not yet have this exciting new feature.

Oregon State Parks were very progressive, and many of the campgrounds even had full hookup sites. We would rumble into our site, and Dad would hook us up to water, electrical, and sewage. Then we were all free to take showers, use the toilet, waste electricity, and leave lights on with impunity. It was sheer luxury compared to our primitive days of tent camping or crowding into undersized trailers.

But when we headed further north, we soon learned that the State of Washington was not as progressive as their southerly neighbor. After several days of camping, our tanks were full, and our father began to search in vain for a place to deposit our repulsive, now dangerously sloshing black water. It threatened to come splashing back up and out of the poorly constructed plastic toilet.

All around the campground we trundled, then all over the region, looking for a dump station to no avail. What to do? Mom and Dad stopped at a store and bought blue chemical to put down the toilet so we could stand the growing stench. Ugh! It was awful—unbearable. And now, the valve in the base of the toilet pot had stuck in the open position. Good grief! I wanted to get out and walk home.

Finally, Dad succeeded in locating a service station with an RV disposal tank in the back. He got permission to use the tank. No charge with fill-up! Those poor, unsuspecting fools!

We filled up on gas, then slogged our way behind the building, mercifully concealed from public view. Dad confidently hooked up the sewage hose to the motorhome and placed the other end into its destination, the desperately needed dump tank. It was nothing more than a hole in the ground with a pop-top opening. Anyone could manage this, right? After all, Dad had experience now—he had already done it at least once. Mom decided to step out to lend moral support. I knew better and stayed inside, hiding.

Dad opened the exterior black water release valve so the water could flow from the motorhome into the dump tank in the ground. Then it happened; the locking clamps on the hose broke free, and there was a frightening sound of violently rushing water, terrifying in volume. A horrific stench split the air, punctuated by screaming obscenities as my Dad leaped backward to avoid a cascading waterfall of furiously gushing filth.

I heard Mom cry out, "Oh NO! Carroll, what's happened?"

"Dammit, Flora! Can't you see that the f*ing valve has broken loose? Geez, there's shit EVERYWHERE!"

"What do we do, Honey?" Mom pleaded. My dad was stupefied. He simply stared in horror. Mom rushed inside to grab an empty milk carton, then raced back out in vain to try and scrape the rapidly-spreading blanket of chemically enhanced blue goop into the impossibly small hole in the ground. The task was futile. Dad had found a hose and was trying to wash the stuff out of view.

Us kids had come outside to investigate, witnessing a massive carnage scene of blue poop and green, slimy water rapidly streaming around the corner of the building and into full view of shameful discovery.

"Get back into the RV! Everyone! NOW!" Dad screamed.

"But, Carroll, what about the mess?" Mom cried in horror.

"NOW!!" my dad hollered. "Get in NOW, dammit, we're leaving!"

We roared out of there. "I'm too embarrassed to face it," Dad confessed as he raced out of the station, careening on two wheels around the corner and onto the highway.

"Dad, please go back," I implored. "I'll help you." But this plea fell on deaf ears. He was mortified and fleeing in fear. Fight or flight had kicked in, and he chose flight.

So off we went, retreating like criminals. I was horrified as I witnessed my very first, full-scale environmental disaster. The future oil spill of the *Exxon Valdez* in Alaska would pale in comparison.

I think that service station still has a wanted bulletin out with my Dad's picture, and it's been more than fifty years.

Ouch!

In the days that followed, our motorhome adventure worsened. I think the gods wanted their revenge on us for the blue poop incident, because the toilet valve stayed stuck in the open position. I wanted to blame someone. But Mom shushed me and Dad said it was everyone's fault. Finger pointing was pointless.

The rising stench was sickening, and even with the bathroom door shut we could hardly bear it. There were tears in our eyes. Dad tried to pull the valve closed with pliers, but this only cracked the plastic and made the situation worse. We tried taking the motorhome to the repair shop, but no one would touch it—it was too much like a hazmat scenario, I think. There was no choice but to head for home and return the wretched thing to the rental place. And we were a three-day ride away!

"Kids, no using the toilet unless it's an emergency, and then only for peeing!" Dad ordered us. "We are heading home as fast as we can!" Then, as he backed up to pull away from the curb, we heard a loud, screeching, tearing crash! Dad raced outside to see a ten-inch hole in the right rear end of the motorhome, courtesy of a local fire hydrant. The hydrant looked stalwart and vengeful: how dare we bring this stinking abomination into town?

This was just too much! We all expected another shouting fit with my dad kicking tires and perhaps even breaking windows in rage. But, by now my poor father was so inured to our appalling situation that he just shrugged his shoulders in sad defeat. He went into the storage compartment and shuffled around for several minutes. Then he came out with some black electrical tape in his fist. He bent down and taped the word "OUCH!" in bold, capitalized letters around the now gaping hole. It looked so funny!

Then we pulled away from the curb a second time. People on the roadway were pointing, laughing, waving, and honking their horns at us all the way home. We had become unlikely celebrities: RV road warriors dragging their sorry butts back down the long holiday road to home.

The next morning the shower curtain ripped off the rods, and a burner almost caught fire on the kitchen stove. Dad could not drive home fast enough. We traveled long hours into the night, stopping only to sleep for a few hours in roadside rest areas, with the sounds of freeway traffic blasting and bellowing in our ears. But, eventually, we made it home and raced off to the sanctuary of our rooms where we could breathe again. As our nostrils slowly expelled the stench of the open toilet, we joyously relaxed in roomy comfort and clean air.

Dad returned the motorhome the next day. Things did not go so smoothly. There was lots of shouting. At first, it seemed like he would be charged more than $3,000 for repairs. But then, Dad railed at them for the toilet valve.

"Why did the damn valve stick in the open position?" he cried. "Your faulty machine caused us tremendous grief! We had to come home two days early!"

The RV shop managers backed off a bit in response to Dad's fearsome outburst. There was still the issue of the torn-open metal on the rear end, they said, and the removal of the "Ouch" sign. One of the owners couldn't help laughing. "Okay, Mr. Smith. We will only charge you for the exterior repair."

"Fine," said my dad. "Are you going to refund us for the lost time, since we were forced to return early due to your stinking, stuck toilet valve?"

In the end, Dad was charged only $300. He came home triumphant. I worried there might be a whole new "Wanted" poster out there in all of the RV rental shops for the next twenty years. But, thankfully, this didn't happen.

Are You Kidding Me?

My little sister, Chrisi, remembers a trip along the Oregon coast when we were driving along in our RV on our way to a mail boat ride on the Rogue River. The mail boat service was a method to deliver mail, but they also allowed tourists to ride along to help generate revenue. It was a great way to see the river because the mail boats went upstream as well as downstream.

Dad was in a bit of a hurry because he didn't want to miss our scheduled ride. But it seemed like the whole world was against him on the road that day. First, there were delays on the road. Then there were road closures and detours. He started getting really nervous about missing the boat ride. Now we were going to be late! Perhaps we would still make it, just in time? Then the unthinkable happened: an Oregon trooper car stopped us. Lights were flashing on the trooper car as the officer got out of his vehicle and came toward us.

"Were you speeding, Carroll?" Mom asked?

"No, Flora, I'm sure I was only going the speed limit," Dad replied in horror. How could he have been stopped, especially now, when he really needed to get to our boat ride on time? Dammit!

"What's happening, Dad?" we shouted from the back.

"Quiet, kids! Don't talk!"

"Dad was speeding," Chrisi said joyfully.

"I was NOT speeding, now be quiet!" Dad hollered.

"Carroll, Honey, relax," Mom said, trying to calm his rising angst.

"Good afternoon, sir," the officer said through the window. "How are you and your family today? I just wanted to get a closer look at your rig." The officer walked around to the entry door on the passenger side and waited expectantly to be let inside.

"Why does he want to look at our rig?" Mom asked.

"Dammit, Flora, if I knew I would say so. Maybe it's dragging on one side? I have no clue." Dad was getting exasperated. "Kids, step out of the RV right now so the officer can look inside."

The trooper walked in and took a look around, asking questions about how everything worked. Dad complied and gave short answers, wondering what the heck was going on.

"Thanks for the tour," the trooper said, after a full ten minutes had passed with this inspection. "What did this rig set you back?"

"We rented it," Dad replied. "Why?"

"Oh, well, my family wants to rent a rig just like this one and before I lay down the big bucks for something like this, I want to know a little bit more about it."

"You mean you stopped us just so you could look at the RV? Do you have any idea how much trouble you cost us? We are trying to get to a boat ride and now we are probably going to miss it!" Dad was in full fury. "Can we go now?"

"Sorry, sir, you are free to go," said the trooper as he stepped outside.

Dad got back behind the wheel. "Kids, get back inside right now! We are outta here!" Dad hollered. We barely managed to climb aboard before Dad gunned the accelerator and charged back onto the road.

"Remember the speed limit, sir," shouted the officer as he was enveloped in a cloud of dust.

The mail boat was still there when we arrived at Gold River, Oregon.

We also liked to stop in Oregon at the coastal town of Bandon. It is a quaint little village where the town council had thought to preserve the old waterfront. Brightly painted wooden shops offered unique souvenirs, and visitors could learn all about the local cranberry trade.

We loved walking past the little shops and eating crab and shrimp cocktails at the sidewalk seafood stands next to the bay. This was a truly spectacular part of the coast where striking rock formations called sea stacks tower above the water. Just south of town several public beaches beckoned day trippers to explore the rocky headlands.

We also looked forward to stopping in town at the Bandon Cheese Factory. People were able to watch the cheese-making process through viewing windows of the visitor gallery. It was fascinating to see the different stages involved, and there was also a helpful video on a wall screen that described the process. Patrons could walk around the visitor's gallery and sample all the different kinds of cheese they had for sale: smoked cheddar, garlic-herb, jalapeno, Monterey jack, and a dozen more. They also sold delicious ice cream at a counter.

Small cube-sized pieces of cheese were on display with little toothpicks to pick up the samples. A big bonus was the cheese curd samples, which were tasty, chewy little rounds of cheese with a rubbery consistency. Dad loved this—all of it—but he especially loved those cheese curds.

He strolled up and down the area, snatching cheese samples like a starving patron. He made sure he sampled everything. "Try these, kids, they're great!" he would say, as he grabbed multiple toothpicks of each kind at once. When he got to the cheese curds, there was no stopping him, and he began gobbling them down like a starving man.

"Sir, please," said the saleswoman. "Please enjoy yourself but don't take them all. We need to have enough for everyone."

"What?" My father was flabbergasted. How dare they tell him to stop sampling? Weren't these samples out for the taking?

"We buy a lot of stuff here every year, you know. Don't tell me how many samples to eat! Flora, kids, take some more!" Dad was outraged. He had a shopping basket filled with different cheeses he intended to buy. He was no slouch! He was here spending hard-earned money.

"Honey, let's just buy our cheese and go," Mom said, but now Dad was angry.

"Why should we have to hurry and go? We have just as much right to be here as anyone else!" he said, as he defiantly stuffed more cheese curds into his mouth. Mom became alarmed. She didn't want to cause a scene. She had to drag Dad out of there somehow. She quickly ordered a double strawberry ice cream cone for him and put this into his hands. This was a brilliant tactic on her part. Strawberry was his favorite flavor, and this immediately mollified him.

"Honey, why don't you get the kids into the camper and I'll buy some cheese curds for us to eat on the road," Mom offered. Dad mumbled something incoherent as he swallowed his last handful of cheese curds and stomped outside, ice cream cone in one hand and little Chrisi's hand in the other. I stayed to help Mom pay as we all breathed a sigh of relief. Crisis averted!

In the years that followed, the well-known Tillamook Creamery in Oregon bought out the Bandon Cheese Factory. The Tillamook Valley is about an hour north of Bandon and it abounds with green pastures, dairy cows, lighthouses on rocky promontories, an Air Museum, and the Tillamook Creamery, one of the largest on the West Coast.

The Bandon Cheese Factory was eventually dismantled and completely removed from the site. In its place today is the Face Rock Creamery, founded in 2013. We really miss the old place, which is now only a happy memory.

Rain Forest Reveries

During the summer of 1970, we took a trip to Washington's Olympic Peninsula and spent time in the Hoh Rain Forest. It was one of several rain forest valleys in that spectacular region. I had never been to a rain forest before, and I had thought they only existed in tropical climates. But in the Pacific Northwest, there was an entire region where the annual rainfall was over ninety inches per year.

We had read about Olympic National Park and the Hoh River Valley, an amazing place where a dense canopy of trees towered above the forest floor. Fallen logs sprouted into cathedral-like colonnades of new growth. Thick, soft carpets of pea-green moss blanketed the ground, and a profusion of new life filled the crystal-clear rainwater ponds.

The wildlife was amazing. We watched gigantic Roosevelt elk lumber through the campgrounds. Herds of white-tailed deer paused to graze in the nearby meadows, and countless creeks were filled with leaping wild salmon and brook trout. There was water everywhere! I had never seen anything like it, and I was entranced.

Such a wealth of natural beauty! So much to learn about! How could we even begin to take it all in? Where should we start exploring—walk the nearby trails? Which ones? What would we find and where?

The answers came from a national park ranger. His name was Kirk Chance. We were sitting in our campsite that first evening, taking in the natural beauty of the place. Then all of a sudden there was a park ranger, right there in our midst! Never before had I seen a ranger walk right up to our campsite. It was the best! Would we like to come to a campfire talk about Olympic National Park? Kirk was walking through the campground, encouraging park visitors to join him at the nearby campfire circle for a slideshow presentation on the rain forest.

We had just finished dinner, so we dropped everything to join a growing group of equally intrigued campers. A lighted path through the forest led us to an enchanting little outdoor amphitheater where Kirk stood proudly next to a campfire, in full uniform with a Stetson hat. He looked so inspirational. He was the picture of the ideal park ranger, one America should be proud of, as he stood straight and tall. And he joked about how it was so wet there that his campfire would probably go out before the talk was over. We laughed.

Nearby was a movie screen where he would give a slideshow and tell us all about the amazing place we had chosen to visit. As visitors approached, they were greeted with a smile and encouraged to take a seat on the split log benches in the campfire circle.

Kirk's presentation spoke all about life in the rain forests of the Pacific Northwest. He talked about what a rich environment this was, filled with life in a fragile, self-sustaining ecosystem. He spoke about the rain forest and how the Hoh River Valley received over fourteen feet of rain per year. He explained how this ecosystem had been here for millennia, and how the magnificent Sitka spruce, western red cedar, Douglas fir, western hemlock, and other trees lived as a community to provide a canopied shelter for the wealth of wildlife that lived here. We were all intrigued, but none more so than me. It was my first campfire talk given by a park ranger, and I was hooked.

Afterward, the entire group surged forward to talk to Kirk, and he happily greeted them as if they were old friends, smiling, laughing, talking, and sharing stories. There was something about his manner that drew folks to him. He had a folksy manner and seemed to love what he did. It was palpable, and people could feel it. He had park ranger charisma. I would never forget it.

The next day, Nan and I were out on a trail, and we happened upon a guided walk led by Kirk. We looked at each other; should we join his walk?

"Take a chance with Kirk Chance," Nan chuckled. Why not? So we trailed along behind, and we were not the only ones. As others on the trail noticed the little group, they tagged along as well. Soon he had a large following.

Kirk pointed to fallen logs and told us about how these "nurse logs" fed new trees growing on top of them. Suddenly, we became aware of entire colonnades of new trees sprouting from nurse logs all over the forest floor. Kirk explained how this was a complex ecosystem, where all the trees were like a single, living organism growing, developing, sheltering, filtering sunlight, providing shade and cover, and housing innumerable birds, mammals, insects, and a plethora of wildlife. He talked about when a mighty hemlock, spruce, or fir reached its zenith of growth and descended into its elderly years as a standing snag, it still provided shelter for wildlife until it ultimately fell crashing to the earth with a deafening roar, smashing everything in its path. Then the cycle of life began all over as the decaying log provided life to new trees.

No classroom experience ever came close to educating me about the cycle of life as that talk did. I was entranced. Mesmerized. It was so wonderful to learn like this. As he spoke, he encouraged the park visitors' questions, and he thoughtfully answered each query, weaving his answers into the story he was telling. Everyone was so engaged! We all felt so connected. This is what I wanted to do, I realized. This was it! I wanted to become a park ranger!

The Magic Pond

The next day I walked out into the forest, away from campgrounds, trails, people, and civilization. I went in no particular direction, just wandering. I wasn't sure exactly what I was looking for, but I was certain I'd recognize it when I got there. It was an introspective journey, with the soft rain forest sounds all around me.

I walked through giant ferns, across wet marsh grass, and through silent forest glades for about twenty minutes. I was just wandering, really, not sure where I was heading.

Then I saw it through the trees, hidden away, a mirrored rainwater pond. Finding it was like magic—nearly invisible—with no one else around, not even footprints. It was about one hundred feet long and maybe forty feet wide, with a depth of about twenty feet. I could clearly see all the way to the bottom. Crystal clear water flowed through it from nearby creeks. I sat down on the bank, captured by the scene before me. I wanted to take it all in.

The mirrored pond was cast in sunlight and shadow as the light sifted down through the Sitka spruce leaves. I could hear soft bird calls in the meadow beyond, but the pond itself was silent.

Time seemed to slow down. I'd often heard that if a person sat still long enough, nature would come out of hiding. I wasn't waiting, though; I simply sat, just being there in that moment of time. I imagined what it would be like to be a part of that pond. What it would feel like. I wondered who lived there, and what life must be like for them.

I experienced transcendent thought and felt myself inside that pond. I stared deep into its rainwater depths. My thoughts were immersed in it. I was enveloped by its gentle, emerald coolness. It was early evening. Cool, still, silent, and unmoving.

That's when it happened: everyone came out of the shadows at once. Several deer materialized between the trees on the opposite shore. They had been there all along, but now I could actually see them. Birds flitted from trees. Beavers swam toward a dam they were building, with sticks in their mouths. I had never seen a live beaver before. The large one in front looked right at me as it paddled by, only a few feet away. It looked so placid and at home in this quiet microcosm.

Fish leaped from the water, their rainbow-colored scales flashing brightly in the sunlight. A mother duck and eight baby ducklings paddled by under the tree branches. They looked so peaceful, winding left and right. Mountain blue jays landed softly in the branches above me, gently chittering. A few bullfrogs began to croak. Soon, crickets were chirping.

An otter swam by as daylight turned to dusk, deep orange sunlight flashing off the water as the sun slipped into the pond. It was the final movement in the tableau.

I wondered, *Is this what nature really looks like?* We miss so much of life as we crash along at high speed, obliterating opportunities to see the real world in front of us. We rarely see the world as it is.

I love the natural world. I feel out of place in today's world, as though I should have been born long ago, when North America was younger and rain forest places like this stretched all across the Pacific Northwest. On this day, and for this brief hour, I was allowed to be in that other time.

I backed into the twilight shadows, not wanting to upset the quiet peace here. I realized I needed to move slowly and carefully back to camp, or I could get lost in the woods. I eventually retraced my steps and found the path I'd taken in. It was dark when I returned.

"Rosanne, where have you been?" Mom asked as I strolled back into camp. "We were just about to have dinner. We were calling for you. You were gone a long time. We were getting worried."

I tried to tell her about my experience, but she was busy serving dinner from the stove, so I sat down with everyone to eat. Again, I tried to tell them about the pond. No one was listening. I turned to Dad, but he was talking with Gary about fishing. Nan and Mom were talking softly. I realized that this experience was to be my memory alone, over all these years, until I finally decided to tell this story now.

Gary, Me, and the Bear

During our trip to Olympic National Park, Gary and I decided we wanted the full outdoor camping experience. We longed to put up a tent and sleep outside under the stars. No RV camping for us! We wanted to listen to the sounds of the night: crickets chirping, owls hooting, the creek rushing, and the pine trees rustling overhead.

That day Gary and I had been on a hike into the backcountry. We had walked for miles when, all of a sudden, we heard a low, deep, warning growl. Gary said it had to be a bear. I wasn't sure, but we decided it would be a good idea to reverse our direction. We turned around abruptly and headed quickly back down the trail. Gary wanted to run, but I said we had to walk, otherwise a bear will give chase. Fortunately, nothing followed us. But that bear must have decided we were worth investigating, so it waited in the forest and bided its time. Sneaky devil!

That evening we set up our little tent outside, about a hundred feet away from the camper. We were going to have a camping experience! No more being stuffed like sausages into camper bunks! We were sleeping outside in the wild—well, in our campsite, anyway.

It was just a little two-person tent. We put our sleeping bags inside and got everything ready for our big outdoor adventure. We could hardly wait to sleep outside. Later that night, we climbed into the little tent and fell fast asleep underneath a bright canopy of stars.

A few hours later I woke suddenly. Gary was shaking so violently the walls of the tent were trembling. "What's wrong, Gary? Are you cold?" I asked him. "Do you need a blanket?"

"Sshhhh, I think it's a bear, Rosanne," he said in a terrified whisper.

"No way," I said. "Not here in the campground."

"Yes, way," he answered and trembled even harder.

At first, I thought maybe it was a deer, but then whatever it was brushed against the walls of the tent, and then I heard that same, unmistakable low growl. It was a bear! Probably the one we heard on the trail. It must have smelled the cookies in our pockets and followed us.

What to do? If we shouted at it, slapped the walls of the tent, or tried to escape it might attack us. I was afraid, too, because I wasn't sure what creature might be out there. "Gary, don't move. And stop that trembling!" In response to this command, he shook even harder. I didn't think it was possible for anyone to quake this hard. The entire tent was shaking like it was in the midst of an earthquake. "Gary, try and settle down. Whatever it is will lose interest and go away," I said. His eyes wide with fright, my poor little brother just stared at me in absolute terror.

I was trying not to act scared too. But that growl was very alarming. It had been my dumb idea to sleep out here, and now we were both going to be attacked, killed, and eaten by some bear. I put my arms around Gary and whispered in his ear to be still, assuring him that the bear would go away.

We heard some shuffling around the campsite, and some more low growls and grunts as it investigated the area. A couple of tin cups on the picnic table were scooped up and then crashed to the ground. A moment passed and then we heard some crunching and scraping sounds. The grilling tools left in the campfire were being sampled. We were glad it wasn't us. Then we heard some more shuffling and grunting, and another loud crash as it knocked over a coffee pot. We couldn't believe Mom and Dad were sleeping through all this. Gradually, the growling moved away as the bear went on to investigate other sites.

When I was sure it was safe, I reassured Gary and stepped outside. It was dark. I couldn't see anything, until I looked up. Never in my life had I seen a more brilliantly lit sky. The entire Milky Way filled the heavens. It was spectacular! There were millions of impossibly bright stars against an inky blackness—so many I could hardly believe it. And the silence—it was amazing. I wanted to become an astronomer.

Growing up in the San Francisco Bay Area, we saw very few stars because of all the light pollution. But here, it was magnificent. I was spellbound. I forgot all about everything: the bear, Gary, the fact that I was freezing cold—everything.

Finally, Gary asked in a frightened whisper, "Rosanne, are you there? Is the bear gone?"

"Yes, Gary, it's gone. Do you want to stay in the tent or go back to the camper?"

"I want to stay in the tent." He surprised me with his answer.

"Are you sure?" I asked.

"Will the bear come back?" he wondered out loud.

"I think we're alright now, Gary. You should come out here and look at the night sky." No answer. "Gary?" I peeked in the tent. He was sound asleep.

Hey, Quit Kicking Me!

My little sister, Chrisi, was born in 1970, when I was sixteen years old. In many ways, she was like my own kid. I took care of her a lot. When we were out in public, people thought she was my baby, especially when I pushed her in the stroller. I had always looked older than my years, so it was common for people to think I was her mom.

Dad and Mom wanted to rent one of their famous family camping rigs for a trip to the British Columbia coast. By now, I was seventeen and getting too old for this. I preferred to stay home. I knew that conditions would be extremely cramped now that we had little Chrisi too. It was bad enough before with the five of us, but with six? Why the heck couldn't we stay in a nice, comfy lodge like most families did?

"We are going CAMPING!" my dad said with booming authority in his voice. "We are not the kind of saps that stay in hotels!" Camping families apparently never stayed in lodges; they were destined to enjoy the wilderness by suffering like cramped sardines in dumpy little rigs designed for Lilliputians.

I wanted to stay at home so badly and just skip the whole darn thing. I was practically an adult. I looked twenty-one, and I had most of the responsibilities of an adult already: a job, school, housework, and constant childcare for my siblings. I even helped out by paying rent, instead of collecting a lavish allowance like most of my friends did. Why must I accompany my family on a camping trip AGAIN? This was a hellish penance indeed, and for what terrible sins, I could not fathom.

There was no way out. My dad would not leave me home alone while they drove hours away on a long-distance trip. Why wouldn't they trust a seventeen-year-old girl alone at home? I wondered. What heinous crimes did they think I would commit?

To his credit, Dad rented a big RV, so there would be more room. I was allowed to sit in front, in the co-pilot's chair. This mollified me somewhat. Mom was relegated to the back for once, stuck with my scrambling siblings.

Things went alright for the trip that first day out. We all had plenty of room to roam around as we rolled down the highway. Dad even offered me a cigarette about an hour into the drive. I smoked one, just to irritate my mom, letting it dangle casually in my hand. I wanted to seem grownup. She protested, but not much. She knew I didn't really like smoking, and I knew it was stupid, so I stubbed it out when I couldn't get a rise out of her. I looked around for snacks instead.

"What do we have to eat?" I asked her as she struggled with Chrisi, who was always wriggling. Mom fished out crackers and that squeezable cheese that comes in a can.

"Don't make a mess up there," she said.

"I want some!" shouted Gary.

"No!" we all hollered, knowing he would suck it all down in three seconds.

"But I'm hungry!" he said. He was always hungry.

Gary was growing up at an alarming rate. He ate everything in sight, like I did. I had always eaten like a food-crazed monster. I loved food. All food. Truck drivers, farm boys, and high school football players ate less than I did. To say that I had a huge appetite would be an understatement. When we went out for pizza, I had to have my own large pizza. I ate day and night. I felt starved in between meals.

But now I had competition. Serious competition. I actually became quite worried there wouldn't be enough food once Gary started growing up. He ate like a maniac. He could snarf down half a chicken when he was six. By the time he was ten it was whole chickens, entire casseroles, two-layer cakes, gallons of ice cream, boxes of cookies—gone in a matter of seconds—nothing was safe from his voracious appetite. And no wonder, since he later grew up to be six-feet four and 220 pounds.

Setting up camp and having dinner that evening was reasonably peaceful. We just rolled into our site. No drop-leaf clamps, no setting up awnings, no carrying water in buckets. We were modern and self-contained. Once again, we marveled at the technological convenience of RV living. It was wonderful. Our own bathroom with a shower and toilet—no more sharing noisy camp restrooms! No stinky Coleman stove or hissing Coleman lantern. Electric lights and a built-in gas cooktop! An oven, a real fridge, and running water. Amazing!

I had always liked the idea of tent camping and would get my fill of that later as a fully-fledged adult on my own. I was actually somewhat embarrassed at the fact that we were in this noisy contraption with a loud generator, rudely disturbing the peace of our tent-camping neighbors. I just hoped the toilet valve behaved itself this trip.

When bedtime came, revolt broke out. I had staked out the over-cab bunk bed as my own. It was nice and roomy, and I thought it was my due. After all, I was Mom's best helper. But Mom had other plans.

"Rosanne, we need you to sleep with Chrisi tonight," she informed me. "You take the dinette bed by the window and keep her close."

"WHAT? Mom, I don't want to do this. She's a baby and she kicks like a mule. It will drive me nuts," I objected.

"Rosanne, your mother needs to get some rest," Dad admonished. "She has had a long trip today, and you got to ride up front, so just do as you're told."

"It will be alright, Honey," Mom promised. "She'll fall asleep quickly."

I looked dubiously at Chrisi and knew this would not be the case. She had a very naughty look in her eyes. She was notorious for getting up *after* she was put to bed. She liked to roam around and get into trouble, and I did not want to be responsible for her, even though she was just a baby. But there was no use arguing. No one would listen to me. Nan and Gary got stuffed into the over-cab bunk I had coveted, while Mom tucked Chrisi snugly into bed and ordered me to watch her for the night. Dammit.

Good grief! How did I get stuck with this? I wondered. This was absolutely the last family camping trip I would ever go on, I swore to myself. Unfair. Wrong. Not Okay. This sucked! I looked down at the tiny lump that was my baby sister and knew this would be no easy assignment. I briefly considered knocking on the doors of some neighboring camps and begging for a free bunk like some hapless refugee.

With a big, deep sigh I climbed into the bed with Chrisi. She was asleep, so I put as much distance as I could between us. I just wanted to rest. But, of course, she immediately began kicking the hell out of me. And she was sound asleep. Why would someone kick like this while they were sleeping?

No wonder Mom wanted out. The more I moved away, the harder she kicked. Kick, kick, kick! "Stop it," I whispered. No response. Silence for several minutes. Ahhh, she's settled down, I thought, and started to drift off to sleep. Then, more kicks. Kick, kick, kick! Little feet kicking, little arms reaching, feeling for a body to latch onto. Yet she was asleep. "Chrisi, quit kicking," No response.

She looked serene; her little face was set in beatific repose. I moved away. Again, I began to drift toward blissful sleep, dreaming of a huge, soft, endless bed all to myself. It was a lovely dream and then kick, kick, kick. Would this go on all night? I wondered. She was driving me nuts. "Stop kicking, Chrisi!" She scooted closer. I pushed her away. Again, she scooted closer. This was ridiculous, I thought. She was relentless. Push away, scoot back. Push harder, scoot closer. She was like some hideous parasite. An absurd snuggle monster. She was asleep, alright, but she was determined to attach herself to me or else kick mercilessly all night. I gave up. I pulled her close. She immediately fell motionless and did not budge the rest of the night. That was all she wanted, to be snuggled close. I'm never having kids, I thought, as I finally fell asleep. Chrisi slept like an angel, the little monster.

Who Threw That Rock?

We made our way up the Oregon and Washington coast to Port Angeles, where we drove right onto the ferryboat that would take us to the British Columbia coast. The ferryboat ride was spectacular! Tall, snow-capped peaks cascaded down to the deep blue waters of the long, narrow channel of the Inside Passage. I was spellbound. I stood up on deck leaning out over the rails. I wanted to continue all the way up to Alaska. What natural wonders awaited, I wondered? It was so breathtakingly beautiful!

We arrived at our port and trundled into Victoria, British Columbia. It was fun looking around the shops and having a teatime lunch at the impressive Empress Hotel. But I was keen to continue north to our camping place in a provincial park in British Columbia. That was in the early 1970s. Resources were incredibly rich there at the Sunshine Coast.

Streams were flush with fish, and prolific oyster beds lay a few steps from the estuarine beaches. There was a tremendous wealth of shellfish free for the taking; clam digging yielded buckets full of fist-sized mollusks.

Wildlife abounded all around with bear, elk, deer, fox, moose, otters, seals, sea lions, and countless other marine and land animals. Overhead and all around was an abundance of birds including bald eagles, pelicans, golden eagles, egrets, great blue herons—I had never seen anything like it. Emerald forest lined the Pacific shore.

I knew that California had once been this way, with magnificent redwood groves reaching all the way to the ocean and salmon so rich and plentiful you could walk across the water on their backs when they swam upstream to spawn. The skies would darken with the shadows of millions of migrating birds, and myriad rich plant life was everywhere. To see such a wealth of resources here stunned me. I knew it couldn't last. But I loved seeing it then and appreciated it all the more.

We walked out to a nearby stream that meandered onto a beach. There was a little pool of water about thirty feet across where trout liked to congregate. Gary, Nancy, and I took pictures of each other holding Chrisi upside down, like she was a huge trophy fish. She looked so sweet, so cute, so adorable in her little sun outfit and colorful derby hat. Great big eyes. Rosy cheeks. Round little face with baby features. Little monster.

My Dad decided to fish there. He was content, standing in the creek, happily hooking brook trout in the sunlit afternoon. All was joyful, right, and well with the world, until we stood Chrisi right side up onto her little sandaled feet.

She had been watching us toss pebbles into the creek, enjoying the deep splooshing sounds they made, and she decided to mimic us. Except that she tried to best us by picking up a huge cobblestone in her little hands, and she hurled it hard. As this mini boulder cannoned through the air, it connected with a loud, cracking thwackkk! It smacked right into the back of Dad's skull! This bone-smashing, unexpected assault stunned him so hard that he lost his balance and fell headlong into the creek with his fishing boots on.

We stared in horrified silence as he roared back up out of the water shouting, "WHO THREW THAT ROCK???" We all pointed to little Chrisi, but my Dad couldn't believe it. How could someone so small hurl a rock that big? And with such force? It had nearly cracked his skull. He was bleeding profusely, and already there was a growing lump on the back of his head the size of an orange. This sudden impact would bother him for years to come.

He looked accusingly at each of us in turn, glaring at us, only to be greeted by stuporous denial. "Rosanne, did you throw that rock? Nancy? Gary?"

Then he looked into the eyes of our baby sister, and she stared back happily at him, with unabashed pride at what she had accomplished.

Dad told me later that he had looked back at her in that moment in dumbfounded disbelief. He finally understood—and the terrifying realization dawned on him—that this was who he would be dealing with for the next twenty years.

My little sister, Chrisi

Dad and Chrisi in British Columbia

Raw Oyster Fever

We had arrived at the beautiful coast of British Columbia only two days before, and my dad was hell-bent on harvesting and pillaging the local natural resources. He had joyously hooked several hapless salmon from the calm waters of the bay, and our family had learned the scoop on clamming. We dug buckets of them up—never had we seen such a wealth of natural resources! There were untold numbers of fish and shellfish.

This was in the early days before people really began discovering Canada as a recreational paradise. We Californians had clearly decimated the fish populations in our own Golden State and now we were heading north like a plague to plunder Canadian waters. Local residents were few in number, so it was still a hunter's and fisherman's paradise.

Dad decided he wanted to get some oysters. His local buddy, Ron, who was our guide, had spoken about a place where there were wild oyster beds, and the delectable shellfish were free for the picking. Ron drove us out over a bumpy dirt track to a spot where you could already see a serious dent had been made in the local oyster population. Still, there was a plenitude. Deep, clear-blue waters. Oyster beds everywhere! And these all grew here naturally. These weren't farm oysters; this was a place where they actually thrived. Unbelievable.

Dad was beside himself with joy. He couldn't believe our luck in being led to a place like this. All across the shoreline were thousands of oysters, so many and so near you could easily wade out to them and fill sacks full—whole boatloads full if you wanted to. This was public land and there was no regulation—at least not at that point in time. Or this is what Ron told us. For all we knew, what we were doing was illegal, and we could be hauled off and arrested. This was a more likely scenario.

Ron launched a small aluminum fishing boat into the gentle water to make the harvesting easier, so we all climbed in. Now we could easily float from oyster to oyster, choosing favorites to pluck and plunder. Dad filled several buckets full.

At one point he realized he was hungry from all the hard work. He decided he wanted to try an oyster on the half shell, right out there on the calm waters of that beautiful bay.

"Here, Carroll, just open one up and slide the oyster right down your throat." Ron handed Dad a shucking knife.

Dad excitedly shuffled through the bucket, pulled out an oversized oyster that looked like a winner, shucked it open, and slurped it right down as we looked on, aghast.

"UGH!!!" we all shouted, as Dad grinned broadly and reached for another.

"Honey, you don't know how those are going to sit with you," Mom softly interjected. "They might make you sick."

"Flora, it's fine," my dad warned her off like a kid with his first piece of candy. Mom looked extremely concerned. Then he slurped another oyster down. And another. And another. "These are so delicious," he said. "Rosanne, come try one of these."

"No way!" I said.

"Ugh!" everyone repeated in unison.

A few moments passed as we surveyed in wonder the idyllic scene around us. Sapphire-blue, calm bay waters. Tall evergreen trees lining the shore. Cloudless skies. Pelicans diving nearby, and a rich plenitude of birds all around. What a paradise!

Then suddenly, Dad's expression changed. His eyes took on a glazed look and his skin took on a sickly, greenish pallor.

"Are you alright, Carroll?" my mom asked, solicitously. "Honey?" No response.

Ron suddenly realized that his formerly enthusiastic fishing companion was now lying down in the boat trying not to be sick. "Hmmm, guess I better get us back to shore," he matter-of-factly stated, as he steered us over to the beach.

Dad slowly clambered out and we all followed him into the car. He remained wordless and we could all tell he was trying his best to maintain on the long, bumpy ride back to camp.

Once there, Mom thanked Ron for our adventure. Then she gently guided Dad inside our camper and got him settled in bed. He slept for the rest of the day.

It would be a long time before I ever decided to try eating oysters.

Strawberry Picking and the Midnight Sun

We loved picking salmon berries. They grew all along the trail into camp. Mom handed us pots and pans and told us to fill them up. These large, pinkish-yellow berries were lovely. Sweet like a strawberry and shaped like a raspberry. They were easy to pick from the six-foot-tall bushes all around us. We picked buckets of them and still there were thousands more, everywhere. We brought them back to the camper and Mom cooked these on the stove to a jam-like consistency. Then she poured a quick baking mix over them and baked them in the oven to make a cobbler. It was delicious. I still couldn't get over the fact that we could simply step outside and collect food like this. What a bounty!

Afterward, Dad built a campfire. We stayed up late talking and laughing in the warm summer air. Because we were so far north, we could enjoy the late sunlight, and marveled at the fact that it could still be light outside after ten p.m. Further north in Alaska the summer sun stayed out all night, barely dipping below the horizon before rising again. It was hard to go to sleep while it was still sunny out, but eventually Mom ushered us all into bed.

As I fell asleep, I thought about our family berry-picking adventures many years before.

When I was about ten years old, we often went to a field near home to pick strawberries. It was a large, open field above the ocean. Nobody really seemed to know or care about this undeveloped patch of land covered with wild strawberry plants.

The field was surrounded by housing developments. We knew that at some point this beautiful spot would face the bulldozers that had already ripped apart peaceful lakes, jade-colored meadows, and coastal marshes rich with wildlife. This would be done in the name of "progress" to build countless, identical little houses.

Strawberries grow naturally along the California coast, so it is possible that these strawberry plants developed on their own. Or perhaps it was a long-forgotten agricultural site, but it didn't have the look of a cultivated field. We had no idea how long it had been there, or exactly how it had come into being, but it was a treasure.

My father discovered the field one day while wandering around the area. We lived in a housing tract nearby. Thousands of homes were being built in the 1950s and '60s as families moved out of rented flats in San Francisco into the nearby suburbs, each with dreams of acquiring homes of their own.

It wasn't surprising that everyone else, as they enjoyed their suburban bliss and their carefully tended lawns, overlooked the lovely strawberry field nearby. But when Dad spotted it one day, in full bloom with thousands of bright red strawberries peeking out from under shiny green leaves, he was thrilled. Undiscovered country! Crimson-hued berries, free for the picking and no one else around! He could hardly believe that such bounty existed just a short distance away from where he lived. Who owned the field? A farmer? Unlikely. There were no fences or signs anywhere. He smiled wide and whistled to himself as he made his way back home.

He burst into the house. "Flora, get the kids! Grab some buckets and pails. We're going berry picking. You won't believe what I found— millions of 'em! No one else around. Free for the picking. C'mon, Honey, let's go!"

"Carroll, what are you talking about? Where is this place? How did you find it? Is this on private property?" Mom asked all the sensible questions.

"Flora, quit worrying. There are no fences. It's open land. There are no signs anyplace."

Dad had concluded, however illogically, that since there were no fences, this open land must be public property. He had no compunction about potential trespassing. Always the sensible fellow.

We all piled into the car with our various berry-picking pails and drove over to the site. It was almost within walking distance. We got there in the evening light, as the sun slanted across the field, throwing shining rays upon the ground. These were wild berries, small and juicy, full of sweetness and flavor. They weren't like the big and comparatively tasteless strawberries you find in the supermarket. Even back then genetically engineered fruit was starting to make a mark. These field strawberries were little, smaller than a thumbnail, and amazingly delicious.

We each had a container to put our berries in: Mom, Dad, Nancy, Gary, and me. We were given free rein to find and pick as many berries as we could. It was an adventure for us to actually go out into nature to seek and gather. We loved it! We would have contests to see who could pick the most. We did this time and again. Dad always managed to pick the most, no matter how hard we tried to best him. We thought he must have a third hand hidden somewhere.

After we drove back home and washed the berries, Mom put them all into a colander to rinse and drain, then placed them into a big bowl. She would make whipped cream, real whipped cream, from scratch. She bought the thick, heavy cream at the grocery store. Then she gradually added vanilla and sugar to it. Next, she whipped it up with her Kitchen Aid mixer. I loved the sound of the mixer whirring. It always meant something good was coming: a cake, pudding, muffins, cookies—or in this case—whipped cream. Mom and Dad would spoon the fresh berries into bowls for each of us, then top them with the cream. Dad would sit proudly back, congratulating all of us on our efforts.

We returned to the field many times, until one day, a horrible disaster struck. As we drove up the hill, we spotted them: ANOTHER FAMILY! They were picking berries in our secret field. How had this travesty happened?

"Flora! The Johnsons are here!" Dad hollered. "How could they come here?"

"How did they learn about this place?" Mom asked. "Did you tell anyone?"

"Well, I guess maybe I did," Dad stammered. "But I didn't expect them to actually come here! Look, their kids all have containers. They're all out here picking our berries. What the hell? There won't be any left for us!"

"Well, Honey, why did you tell them about it?" Mom asked.

Dad didn't have an answer for this. He knew he had no one to blame but himself. He had let the word out. Like anyone who discovers a new treasure, he couldn't keep the secret to himself. But now he was filled with dismay. This other family was stealing *his* strawberries! Just because he had told Bill Johnson about it, that didn't mean he had given him permission to come here, did it? That was privileged information, wasn't it? How could they do such a thing?

"Kids, get out there now and pick some berries!" Dad demanded. "Go on, go get them while there are still some left. I looked around doubtfully. Every Johnson kid had containers stuffed full of berries. I saw no berries left on the now-trampled plants in the ground. I raced around to all my favorite picking spots—nothing. Nothing left, anywhere. Gone, all gone. Thoughtless footprints everywhere. They had ravaged the field. Crushed the plants. It was devastating. Dad had given away our secret and now the field was no longer ours.

"Let's go home," Dad said sadly.

"Are you going to talk to Bill?" Mom asked.

"What's the use? The berries are gone," Dad lamented. We all climbed back into the car with our empty little pails.

"Hi guys!" Bill waved and called to us. Dad ignored his friend as he glowered into the fading light of day. We drove back in silence.

"Carroll, Honey, it's alright. Let's just go to the store and buy some strawberries," Mom offered.

"But it's not the same, Flora." Dad fumed. We bought berries at the store, and he was right, it wasn't the same. These genetically-engineered imposters seemed tasteless in comparison.

We talked of going to the field early the next season before word spread and more families got the idea of going there. We knew the word would soon get out about this particular national treasure.

But the ensuing events were far worse than this. The following year, the dreaded bulldozers arrived to develop a new housing subdivision, and our beloved strawberry patch was replaced by a new crop of houses. No more strawberry wars.

We would have only memories of the field from now on. In the years that followed, all the little dairy farms in the area were also bulldozed for houses. It made me sad. "People have to live somewhere," I was always hearing. Yes, of course they did, but even as a kid, I wished there was a way we could live on the planet without tearing it to bits in the process.

A folk song called *Little Boxes* was written by a woman named Malvina Reynolds in 1962 and popularized by folk singer Pete Seeger in 1963. It characterized suburbia, and the rows of nearly identical little homes on the Daly City hillsides just south of San Francisco's Ocean Beach. This was a place where everyday families could afford to buy a postage-stamp-sized lot with a little house on it, thus stepping into the ranks of proud homeowners. These plain homes all looked the same: Little Boxes. We lived in one of these, too, and I often worried that I would go around the block and get lost trying to come back home again, not knowing which one was the correct house to return to. Lost forever in a suburban tract!

I longed to live in a place where there were evergreen trees, paths to the beach, green meadows to run in, and trails to walk on. I vowed that when I grew up, I would never live in a suburban forest. I wanted to live and work in wild spaces. But how would I do this, I wondered?

Give a Show, Girl

Have you ever been asked, "What is the greatest gift you ever received?" Most of us will immediately think of a loved one, a new home, our first car, an exciting opportunity, or something else that was life-changing for us. Some of us will think back to our childhood and perhaps remember a favorite holiday gift we received.

My favorite gift as a kid was my Give-A-Show Projector. This was a simple, hand-held, battery-powered projector with a slot for cartoon slide cards. The projector was about ten inches long and made of bright red plastic. Each slide card was a seven-picture, mini cartoon strip with printed narration lines at the bottom. (You can still find these as collector's items today on eBay.)

As a nine-year-old kid, I had seen this advertised on TV and I dreamed of thrilling my friends with cartoon shows punctuated by my witty repertoire. I had visions of excited audiences filling a room, delighting in my narrations, and following my presentations with rapt attention.

Christmas time came and I shook all of the boxes under the tree to try and discern if one of them might contain this most cherished of all gifts. I found one that I thought might be the right one. On Christmas morning I opened it, and there it was. I was thrilled!

Now I was all set; I could give a colorful slideshow anywhere. On the walls, on the ceiling, on a sheet, or under the covers! The only problem was, no one wanted to watch. Oh sure, I could lure family and friends up to my room with the promise of snacks and treats, and they would come watch for a few minutes. But soon their eyes glazed over with boredom, and they would sneak out with the treats stuffed in their pockets. Occasionally a good friend might stay, but only if I let them take over the show. This was an outrage! They were supposed to let me give the program. Why weren't they acting thrilled, like those kid audiences on television?

Relegated to the ranks of listener, I became bored too. But the desire to present the shows remained. I realized I loved sharing information. Did I want to be a teacher someday? No, not a classroom teacher, but maybe someone who could share ideas in an unusual setting. I liked the nature shows the best.

I realized that to keep an audience interested, the presentation had to be engaging, not static. No one wanted to listen to a boring script. People wanted to interact with what they were seeing, to become a part of the story. It needed to become *an experience*. The more I thought about it, the more I liked this idea.

I kept that toy for many years. I thought a lot about how much I wanted to share stories with others. I thought about how I would prefer to do this outside, like those campfire programs I had seen in parks.

Back then we all watched the *Yogi Bear* cartoons on television. While we were all supposed to identify and empathize with Yogi and his sidekick, little Boo Boo Bear, I found myself empathizing with Ranger Smith. He was always having to chase down Yogi and stop him from stealing picnic baskets from park campers in Jellystone Park. Yogi couldn't resist; the tempting food was right there within reach.

But then, this made me think about the plight of bears. Why were bears coming into campgrounds to steal people's food? I wondered. Television may have made this into a funny, kids' cartoon, but in truth, this was a real-life issue. In the years that followed, as errant bears became a serious problem in the national parks, I began to understand the situation more. Wayward bears were a people problem. I wanted to be like Ranger Smith and help protect the bears and educate the park visitors to be safe around wildlife. Even as a young kid, I was already leaning towards that park ranger hat!

PART TWO

The Road to Ranger Land

Marin Headlands

Years later, I was a student majoring in geology at San Francisco State University when I saw a notice on the door of a professor's office: "Anyone interested in working with the National Park Service please see me." This was the break I was hoping for.

I gave this note some very serious thought. Could a meeting with a college professor really be the way into a park ranger job? This was 1974. It was a very difficult road for a woman to become a ranger. This was still very much a man's field. Many park ranger advertisement bulletins clearly stated, "Men only." Yet, I knew this was what I wanted to do. This would become my life's work. I could feel it.

My college professor was a man. Everyone in a leadership role on this career path was a man back then. I waited a few weeks, fearing rejection if I went in to ask about this opportunity, until finally I just had to know. I made an appointment with Professor Dave. He told me there was a new national park opening up in the Marin Headlands, immediately north of San Francisco. It was a former military reservation on the northwest side of the Golden Gate Bridge.

There was a huge expanse of open land out there, thousands of acres of coastal meadows and valleys, lagoons, estuaries, marshlands, and spectacular headlands cascading down to beautiful, sandy beaches. It was all part of the newly created Golden Gate National Recreation Area, and they were looking for volunteers to come and give guided talks to the public. I would be working with a small park staff at a visitor center. This was located at a remote lagoon beach called Rodeo Cove.

How did someone get to this place? Just north of the Golden Gate Bridge was a little turnoff called Alexander Avenue that took you directly west to the Marin Headlands. Once off the highway you had two choices; turn left and climb up a winding road to rocky promontories with spectacular views of the Golden Gate Bridge and San Francisco, then wind your way down to the beach; or go through a mile-long tunnel, emerge into a long, narrow valley, and follow the road out to the beach. This was the faster route with less chance of getting lost amongst the maze of military roadways crisscrossing the place.

As the road crested the final hill it bridged a deep lagoon that joined the ocean at Rodeo Beach. This was a wild place with crashing waves and rocky headlands. The sand was the size of pea gravel, multi-colored with jade, jasper, carnelian, chert, and other semi-precious stones. Park visitors were always on the beach, even in the worst of weather, combing the sand for gemstones.

It was an amazing place to work. High coastal ridges reared up to the north and south. Roadways carried one up to dizzying heights atop headlands and rocky promontories. Cliffs plunged down to the ocean. Some curves in the road were treacherous, with hills that dropped down hundreds of feet. A wrong turn could send you tumbling over the edge. The cerulean Pacific Ocean glittered in the sun, luring drivers to look downward as they careened around precarious cliffs. I nearly drove over the edge a few times as I gaped at the majestic views.

At different points along the roadway were World War II gun emplacements, towers, tunnels, and big, circular long-range cannon carriages. There was even an underground Nike missile silo built in the 1960s. Anyone interested in military history would have a field day here. It wasn't my particular expertise; I preferred nature. But this was intriguing to a lot of park visitors, especially those who had served in the military. Coastal defense was extensive here.

There were so many places to step out and explore! One road led to Point Bonita Lighthouse. A little gem perched on a rocky promontory easily visible from San Francisco, it invited visitors for a closer look. A trail of steps led to the lighthouse. The roadway eventually twisted its way back down to the beach.

I was given the name of a man to contact who could fill me in on the details. His name was Tim, and he was the supervising ranger there. "Would this lead to an actual park ranger job?" I asked my professor.

"I think they already have paid staff and are just looking for volunteer help, but that could lead to valuable job experience," he said.

Well, what did I have to lose? I thought. Everyone wanted to be a park ranger back then. It was considered the ideal job. Hard enough for a guy to break into the ranks, but for a young woman, this was not going to be easy. Still, I felt optimistic.

I called Tim the next day at the Marin Headlands Visitor Center. This was a little building out at the beach in Rodeo Cove, one of many ex-military buildings in long rows there. The entire area was once a huge military reservation and the U.S. Army still occupied many of the nearby structures.

The fifteen-by-twenty-five-foot entry room comprised the visitor center, with a big picture window, a few tables with maps, brochures, and objects like sea shells, rocks, and books for park visitors to look at. Maps and posters covered the walls around the room. There were two adjacent offices and a small restroom on the left side. The building faced Rodeo Lagoon and Rodeo Beach; we could watch the ocean waves crashing right onto the sand.

Tim met with me and two other potential volunteers that weekend. He explained that we would be expected to help out every Saturday and on some Sundays. We were to develop and lead guided walks on park natural history and work in the visitor center answering questions. Would we be given resources to help us develop these guided talks? we asked. Tim pointed to a small library of books on a nearby shelf that referenced the natural history of the area. Not a lot to work with, but as a college student, I was pretty resourceful and used to finding answers.

Tim had already hired several other permanent staff, all experienced park rangers and all men. I wondered where they had come from, and how they managed to get here before me. They had already worked in different national parks. One of them, Reeve, had also worked in California state parks.

"What do you feel you have to bring to this job?" Tim asked. "What sets you apart from other volunteers?"

I told him about my experience teaching geology lab classes as a student assistant at San Francisco State. I wondered if I should tell him about my Give A Show Projector days. I was working on a bachelor's degree in geology. My only other experience consisted of working in a bookstore, and some real crummy jobs at convenience stores and a pizza parlor. There was also a two-year stint as a bus girl in a Chinese restaurant which had been ghastly, but I figured this wouldn't help at all. I was still too young to have a lot to offer.

"Well, we'll give you a chance," Tim said.

They must really be desperate for volunteers, I thought.

After the initial meeting and walk-around tour I said I would be happy to volunteer. If nothing else, I could gain on-the-job experience that could lead to an actual job later, and some parks around the country were starting to hire women seasonal rangers. It was still an uphill challenge, but I really liked the idea of working there.

The other students balked at the idea of volunteering that much time and didn't come back. But this was something I really wanted to do. Where should I begin? I wondered. I began to plan a beach walk about the geology of the Marin Headlands. But first, I needed to learn more about the job and who I would be working with.

Me as a national park ranger, Rodeo Beach, Marin Headlands

The Crew

I really loved the work and looked forward to it. I got to know the staff and eventually learned how to give their presentations as well. The men were all so uniquely different from each other and were very likable.

Tim, our supervisor, had light brown hair, blue eyes, and a medium build. He wore glasses and paid a great deal of attention to detail. He expected us to keep logs of everything we did. Tim liked to hold meetings and make plans for the future.

One day, Tim surprised me by offering me a seasonal appointment as a park ranger at Marin Headlands. I had been volunteering for about six months. I was so grateful and thrilled. I had not expected this, and to be invited to join the ranks of the other park rangers was exciting for me. I immediately ordered my first uniforms. I felt so fortunate. I didn't have to apply for park ranger jobs all over the country in places I'd never heard of. Instead, I could work at Marin Headlands, close to home in a place I loved.

Now I had to demonstrate that I could do the full job. I started to go out on more patrols.

We had a lot of latitude in how we did our jobs. This was a generalist ranger position. We performed vehicle, mounted, and foot patrols of the Marin Headlands, which stretched across several thousand acres from the valleys to the beaches, and up to the ridgetops. We also did cliff rescue, first aid, fire support, resource management, and many other tasks. I liked the challenge of doing such a wide variety of duties. I soon began to work with the other staff to get to know them better.

Lloyd was a big, burly, pipe-smoking guy with a full beard and an easy smile. He was the resident expert on military history. Full of anecdotes about how to make a talk interesting, he taught me how to take visitors on guided walks through the old World War II gun emplacements and the 1960s underground Nike missile silo. Park visitors seemed to be fascinated with this subject. The entire region was heavily developed for cannon and missile defense dating back to the Civil War and the Spanish Presidio days. Lloyd also knew a lot about birds and mammals and let me stand in on his tours with him.

My expertise was geology, and there was plenty to talk about with the immense rock formations in that area. I was intrigued and wanted to learn more about everything.

"C'mon, Rosanne, we're going to learn about how to make plaster castings of animal prints today," Lloyd said. "Just grab that bag of plaster and I'll get a jug of water. We'll walk over to that hill where a lot of critters come out at night in search of food. I know we'll get some good prints there, and you can use these for the children's programs." Lloyd had all kinds of anecdotes about how to keep people interested.

We brought these castings back to the visitor center for kids to look at. "Look, Mama, a raccoon print!" kids would say. "Wow, a mountain lion track!" they would exclaim in wonder. It was a great idea.

Reeve was serious and funny at the same time. Dark-haired with a big mustache, he was great at natural history and especially birding. He was also a genius at cliff rescue training. He was a great organizer and a take-charge kind of guy. He knew a lot about the area. A no-nonsense person with a quick temper, Reeve didn't let anyone tell him what to do. I admired his style. He was a hard worker and didn't put up with slackers. He'd be the first one to tell a co-worker to get up off their butt and get to work.

"Quit sitting around at that desk and get outside! Look at all those park visitors on the beach. Are you going to tell me that the report you're doing is more important than going out there right now? That paperwork can wait."

I had no problem with this kind of thinking. Later in my career when I became a manager, I led many staff meetings. But I always made sure these meetings were brief, productive, and to the point.

Reeve hated staff meetings, and after thirty minutes of sitting around talking he would just stand up and head for the door. If Tim tried to stop him, Reeve would say, "Talk, talk, talk, talk, talk. That's all we ever do. Let's just go outside and do our jobs. We aren't here to sit around in damned meetings! We're here to protect the park and talk to our visitors."

This always made me laugh because I loathed staff meetings. And he was right, we weren't there to sit inside and have endless discussions about park policies. We were supposed to be out greeting the public. And with that, the pointless meeting would end. I was grateful.

Mick was tall, slim, and blonde. He looked like the classic textbook ranger of the times. He knew a lot about how to manage our small stock of park horses, and soon I was riding the trails with him. He was a quiet, soft-spoken guy. And he had a good, folksy singing voice that kept the horses calm on the trail. He was easygoing and got along well with everyone. Mick avoided conflict, and I never heard him say an unkind word about anyone. He seemed comfortable doing any job and seemed happiest by himself. I could certainly respect that. I was a loner too and preferred to work by myself. If confronted with an argument over something, Mick would say, "It's not important enough to get angry about. I'm sure you're probably right in your thinking on that." Then he would head for the door.

I was glad to learn about riding from Mick because our park horses would bolt at the slightest sudden move, and he always knew how to calm them down. These horses had been donated to the park. There were two quarter horses named Buster and Indy and, later on, a Morgan named Jack. Based on their extremely skittish behavior, it was a no-brainer that they had been abused. They managed to buck off, kick, smash, and/or injure every single one of my co-workers. For some reason, I managed to escape injury, but only just. I once got between Indy and the corral fence as we were saddling up the horses, when he suddenly got frightened and reared up. I barely ducked out of harm's way as he crashed against the gate, his hooves flying just inches from me. It was a close call. I could easily have been kicked in the head. I grabbed the reins and talked him down, "Calm down, buddy. It's alright; no one is going to hurt you." Neither of us was harmed, thankfully.

Another time Buster reared up and started bucking hard when we were riding down a steep portion of the trail. He had seen something, and it frightened him. I managed to grab the saddle horn and stay on, but I almost got thrown onto the rocks.

Those horses would jump at a piece of paper fluttering along the trail. I found that when they got scared like this it was best just to keep my head and try to reassure them in a quiet voice. Eventually, they calmed down. Then I'd dismount and talk to them, gently running my hands along their beautiful manes and telling them I meant no harm. They were all beautiful animals and responded to kindness, as any creature would. I felt badly that they had been mistreated so much in their past. At least they had a good home now.

Murray was another ranger in our group. Medium height with a strong build, brown hair, and blue-eyes, he was great with visitors. As I watched his interactions with others, I learned how to become more engaging. He told a lot of funny stories and was always kidding around with everyone. This was a real talent. Whenever I tried telling jokes, no one laughed. Instead, they looked at me in puzzled silence at the end of a joke. In fact, people tended to laugh when I *didn't* want them to. This was disconcerting; why wasn't I funny? I felt like a dope trying to kid around, and eventually decided to keep it serious for everyone's sake.

But Murray really knew how to put people at ease. He liked to lead day-long hikes into the neighboring Tennessee Valley. There was a beautiful beach there. Good idea, I thought; lead a day hike and be away from the office. Pretty smart. Why stay indoors answering the phone when you could be outside all day with a group of happy people? I was obviously doing something wrong, or I would be leading day hikes to Tennessee Beach too. I filed this thought away for future consideration.

I vowed to learn more about how to find the perfect ranger job with maximum freedom. How did one go off and escape the watchful eyes of one's superiors? Could it be that easy? I thought not; usually these kinds of behaviors tended to backfire at some point. No one escapes scrutiny for long. But still, whenever I saw a chance for an assignment that offered some autonomy, I jumped at it.

In short, I learned as much as I could about anything and everything. They were a good group of people to work with. Tim was difficult to understand, but I attributed this to the fact that he was very young and was in the unenviable position of being in charge of four other guys who were older, wiser, and far more experienced than him. And they constantly reminded him that they knew more than he did. Tim said little when they did this; he just kept trying to lead. I learned from this example too; a good leader listens to their staff and tries to lead from the front, not the sidelines.

We were joined later by another ranger, Dan. Tall, dark-haired, lean, and fun to be around, Dan was always smiling. He was very kind-hearted and always relaxed. I envied him his disposition. He never seemed to worry about anything. He was also a good rider, so we often patrolled together.

"Don't get so worked up about things, Rose," he'd tell me when I'd get frustrated over conflicting management directives. "It does no good to worry, and most of the time it isn't that important."

"But, Dan, don't you get upset when we are told one thing by Tim and then a higher-up says to do something different?" I'd ask.

"Nope," Dan would smile. "I just go out and do the job the way Tim tells me, and I don't worry about the rest, including Tim," he'd laugh. "Why worry? You have a great job. Just go out and enjoy it and try to forget about what the executives are doing. Our job is here, in the field." Sounded like good advice to me.

The following year, Dan was hired into the Ranger Intake program, the much sought-after full-time career training program for national park rangers. I was happy for him.

We were all expected to learn first aid and CPR. One day we gathered in a little training room at Fort Point National Historic Site, a Civil War-era installation tucked away under the south end of the Golden Gate Bridge, to learn CPR. The CPR dummy we used for practice was so old and moldy she whistled back at us when we blew rescue breaths into her mouth. She reeked of decay. She had streaks of cracked green mold around her lips. She reminded me of one of those ancient fortune-telling dummies in a glass booth where you put a coin in and a crone-like figure clad in colorful garb nodded at you, waved her hand over some tarot cards, and popped a fortune card at you through a little slot.

I kept expecting one of those little fortune cards to drop from the CPR mannequin's moldy fingers. "Get out of here and go away!" it would read, or perhaps, "Begone! A curse on you all!"

When we blew into her lips, she expelled a strange "haroooo" sound that sent us all into uncontrollable spasms of laughter. I had tears in my eyes from laughing so hard. Even though our instructor said it was no laughing matter, who could help it when her exhalations sounded like the distant whine of a deranged ghost?

Somehow, we managed to get trained and certified in spite of our plastic tormenter. I think she spit at us when we weren't looking. It was hard work. After this all-day, intensive course, I went home totally exhausted.

I feared my own lips would turn green and my face might crack open with some alien mold. I had strange dreams that night of being chased around a dark fort by a plastic witch shouting "haroooo!" at me. I woke up in a panic, certain that my face had fallen off. But somehow, I survived the ordeal.

You're Not a Real Cop!

My favorite times were patrolling around a big, bowl-shaped area called the Gerbode Preserve. The six-mile loop trail began near a marsh with a little creek, then it opened into a big meadow on the valley floor. Marsh wrens and redwing blackbirds trilled their songs through the tall grasses and wildflowers. Monkey flower and California poppies were abundant on the canyon walls and on the valley floor, along with patches of skunk cabbage, coyote brush, and poison hemlock. In the spring, there were wildflowers everywhere: wild onion, paintbrush, lupine, columbine, and tiger lilies.

A large stand of eucalyptus trees stood at the base of the ridge and challenged you to ascend to the surrounding hillsides above. From here, the trail wound upward, climbing toward the nearby ridgetops. It took effort to wind your way up that long hill, but once you were on top you were greeted with stunning vistas of the blue Pacific Ocean, the orange-red towers of the Golden Gate Bridge, the impressive San Francisco city skyline, and the entire Bay Area. Up here, you felt as though you were on top of the world.

Some days I walked, and other days I rode horseback. Along the way I greeted visitors and answered questions about the park. I kept field guides in my daypack and often pulled these out to help identify plants and wildlife. The vast majority of people were great stewards of the park, and they loved being outdoors in this beautiful place. Sometimes they would ask trail directions. Many of them just wanted to say hello and asked about how to become a park ranger.

"How'd you get this job? What do you rangers do out here? Do you get to live here? Can I try on your hat?" and so on.

Occasionally, I would discover people driving off road, chopping down trees, letting dogs run off leash, starting wildfires, shooting guns, or engaging in other acts of general stupidity. I wasn't a law enforcement ranger at that time, so I often had to bluff my way through these contacts to stop these unwelcome behaviors. Usually, my uniform looked authoritarian enough to convince people to behave.

But if someone persisted, I had to radio for the U.S. Park Police. I always hated doing this. These officers were stationed at Fort Mason in San Francisco. It took them a minimum of forty-five minutes to get from San Francisco across the Golden Gate Bridge, through the long tunnel, down through the valley, then up a long gravel road to where I stood. By the time they arrived the perpetrators were long gone, causing trouble elsewhere. There was little point in calling the police and every reason to try and bluff my way through each contact as gracefully as I could.

I would calmly tell visitors that having their dogs run wild off leash was a federal offense that could result in a big fine. "Why can't my dog run off leash?"' they would ask, used to having their animals run free. I explained how this could be damaging to wildlife. Or that driving off road could lead to jail and imprisonment, not to mention the fact that this tore up the fragile landscape. This generally worked pretty well.

But there was the occasional person who observed that a real law enforcement officer would have a gun. "You're not a real cop. A real cop would have a gun," a challenger would say. Whereupon I asked them if they preferred to be cited or arrested by the police when they arrived, or to talk to me now and simply follow the rules.

"Uh, okay," they'd say, after thinking this over. Most people complied at this point. But the unlucky few who continued to act like idiots were held to answer by the police who came all the way out to reprimand them. Of course, some got away, but not many. We took our jobs seriously and tracked these perpetrators down.

I was never afraid during these contacts because I had a lot of confidence. But I often felt frustrated that I didn't have law enforcement authority, especially when I saw things happening, like people free-climbing on steep rock faces without proper climbing equipment, illegal cooking fires, illegal plant harvesting, artifact hunting, and other crimes.

Years later, I would become a law enforcement ranger, and it felt good to stop law breakers right in their tracks. I always tried quiet discussion and reasoning first, but if someone persisted in acting poorly, I had the ability to stop bad behaviors quickly with a citation or an arrest. I always wore full gear (handgun, pepper spray, handcuffs, baton, bullet-proof vest, and radio). Being a full peace officer provided me with the authority I needed to stop crimes and protect park visitors and park resources. It was a relief to be able to protect people from wrong behaviors in the right manner, and I never abused this authority.

Wildlife Tales

A lot of times funny things happened. Once, a skunk family decided to take up housing in one of the old World War II gun tunnels. Park visitors reported that their teenage son had been walking around inside, hollering just to hear his voice echo. Then he stumbled upon a skunk family and received a full dose of skunk spray.

These gun tunnels are massive, long, and multi-leveled, with many side chambers and openings in the floor that were formerly used to store munitions. These made great hiding places for wildlife. All kinds of creatures wandered in, and some took up temporary housing. Consequently, you never knew what you might come face-to-face with.

I was asked to go investigate this skunk attack. I was not particularly anxious to do this. I had a healthy respect for all wildlife and preferred to observe them from a safe distance. I did not want to investigate a skunk family at close quarters. This is not quite what I imagined doing when I signed up as a ranger, I thought. This must fall under that ambiguous phrase of "other duties as assigned."

I asked Lloyd to come with me to help me spot the skunk before it spotted me. Those tunnels were dark inside, and I did not fancy getting skunked myself. Better to have one of us to hold the light and the other one to look ahead.

First, we met with the family of the teenage boy to learn more about the situation. "He is covered with skunk spray," the parents lamented as they described what had happened and where the animal was located. "He was just walking along in the dark, yelling to hear his voice, and suddenly he was attacked by skunks, ugh!" the boy's mom told us.

The sprayed boy had learned a valuable lesson: leave wildlife alone! Lloyd had excellent anecdotal information for the mother about how to remove the spray once they got home. They told us approximately where the skunk family was located, deep in the tunnel and down in a hole toward the north end. Then they departed with all the car windows rolled down. The teenage boy looked quite subdued and miserable. Poor kid!

We decided to mount a rear attack and enter the tunnel from the back side so we could sneak up on the skunks before they spotted us. We weren't exactly sure where they were, so we had to tread carefully. We whispered as we walked through the cavernous maze. About one hundred feet in Lloyd said, "Stop now, Rosanne. Don't walk any further." As he said this, we swept our flashlights across the floor. A mother skunk and her babies were right near my feet! They were in a small opening in the ground about three feet below me. I froze in shock and then backed up slowly. The alarmed skunk started spraying, but because it was in a confined space it couldn't zap me, although it sure tried. But the stench was almost overpowering. From a distance, skunk spray isn't too bad. It smells a lot like coffee brewing. But up close—YIKES! My eyes watered. I could hardly breathe. It was awful! I gagged, and we both made a very hasty retreat. Now I could feel true and complete empathy for that teenage boy. Nothing like firsthand experience to illustrate what nature could spew at you when you invade a territory. It took several moments for me to catch my breath and avoid vomiting right in front of my co-worker. Ugh.

We cordoned off the tunnel from both sides with police tape and went back to headquarters to discuss this with Tim and the other staff. What to do? We called county animal control. They most certainly did NOT favor coming out to remove the skunks. They advised that this was most likely a temporary situation and that, after the mother had raised her brood in a few weeks, they would most likely all depart for the great outdoors. We put up signs at the gun tunnel warning park visitors about the skunk family and to stay out. And, eventually, our striped residents departed for the nearby fields.

Sometimes a stray wildlife visitor would come not from land, but from the ocean.

"There's a big seal on the beach!" we would occasionally hear people say. Rodeo Cove, our little beach near the visitor center, was an area with strong ocean currents and riptides. Waves crashed with a mighty force on the steep beach face, and we often had stray marine mammals landing there. Seals, sea lions, and elephant seals were frequent visitors. Usually lone bulls, they would take refuge on the beach for a few days to rest, then gradually make their way back into the sea once they regained their strength. But others were injured and lay stranded on the beach for weeks.

We often called a marine rescue center in San Francisco to come evaluate the stranded animals. Sometimes they were transported to veterinary help, and other times they were left in place to rest, recover, and return to the sea on their own. In these cases, we cordoned off an area of the beach near the animals to keep people away.

This situation became so frequent that, eventually, a marine mammal rescue center was established in 1975 on a hill near the beach.

In the years that followed, the Marine Mammal Center became a preeminent facility for marine mammal rescue on the West Coast. There are now multiple branches in California, Hawaii, and across the globe.

But when I was there, this was all in its infancy, and our job was to educate the public to leave these stray marine mammals alone. With their big eyes and almost human-like expressions, they were compelling to look at, and people unwittingly wanted to get close to them. This could result in serious injury, as the animals would bite to protect themselves.

It always amazed me how foolish people could be, walking up to these big creatures and wanting to pet them or take photos. "Look, kids, a seal! Let's get some photos with it. Go stand next to it while I take the pictures."

What is it about humans that makes us want to do this? Maybe there are too many films and books that anthropomorphize animals and make people think that all animals are cuddly? I've always had a healthy fear of our planetary coinhabitants and have kept a respectful distance. But some humans are inherently ignorant about this.

So, it became our job to educate people. We gave guided walks along the beach, talking about marine mammals and how important they are to our planet. We did special walks for children. These talks soon became very popular, especially when there was a marine mammal on the beach. We talked about what it would feel like to be in their place, having a lot of humans walking up to you and how stressful this could be for the animals.

Children can be great empathizers, especially when they are able to imagine what something is like and they can give a name to things. Our goal was to educate them to become good stewards of our planet.

"Let's get down onto the sand now, away from the animals, and lie here for a few moments," I would tell them. "You're a little seal and you are exhausted from being in the waves. You're separated from your family. You're afraid. Look at those strange creatures (humans) over there. They don't have flippers, and they walk on those funny-looking sticks (legs) coming out of their body. What do they want from you? Why don't they go away?"

The kids loved lying in the sand imagining this scenario. It really opened their eyes to what it might be like from a marine mammal point of view, and why it is so important to protect them. "I want to be a seal or a sea lion," the kids would say in amazement.

I remember one time when I was told I would be videotaped while giving a talk to a group of very young children. The idea was to self-evaluate how effective our interpretive presentations were. I hadn't developed many talks for little children yet, so this was going to be a big challenge for me. I created an outdoor talk that was designed to engage the kids and get their attention.

On the day of the talk, I don't remember seeing an individual child. Instead, I felt like there was a whirring cloud of kids all around me, and I was pretty sure that no one was paying attention to a single word I said. These were little children, from preschool and kindergarten. I'm not getting through to them, I thought to myself.

Afterward, the video crew and I went back to the ranger station and watched the video of my talk. I was amazed. Those children *had* been listening to me! What had seemed like a whirlwind to me had actually been a flurry of little faces paying rapt attention and taking in nature at the same time. Children learn differently, I remembered. Whatever program we design for them, they need to feel engaged. Children are in constant motion and it isn't realistic to expect them to be still to learn. They actually learn best when they are able to move around, with the teacher at the epicenter of their collective energy. This was quite a revelation for me. From then on, I realized that reaching out to children was critical. They are our future. And they all listen in their own, individual way.

Gemstone Sands! We're Rich!

Rodeo Beach was a spectacular mix of multi-colored, semiprecious gemstones. Bright orange carnelians; deep red jasper; yellow, green, and red chert; green jadeite—it all came from deep down in the San Andreas fault zone. This entire region was a unique slice of geology called the Franciscan Formation. I used to go out and gather up people from the beach and take them on guided geology walks along the shore.

"Want to come along with me and learn about how to look for carnelians in the sand and find out about the geology of this place?" I would ask, enticingly. Carnelians were the semiprecious reddish orange stone everyone looked for there. People would jump up from their beach blankets to learn more.

We would pick up handfuls of the richly colored pebble sand and rhapsodize about its amazing contents. Standing in a little circle with park visitors and hearing the waves crashing around us was the greatest experience.

"Can we get rich if we collect enough of these bright stones?" people would ask.

"Actually, you're not supposed to remove anything from a national park," I explained. Whereupon guilty looks appeared on every single face in the group as they slyly emptied their pockets.

"And I thought we could get rich here!" a little boy said.

"You are incredibly rich," I answered. "Just look at the beauty all around you. This place belongs to all of us."

"It does?" asked the little boy. "Which part is mine?"

"All of it" I said.

"WOW!" he exclaimed.

People were fascinated to learn about how this place was formed. We would walk up onto a nearby knoll looking out over the beach and lagoon, and I would talk about how the Pacific Plate was colliding with and sliding underneath the North American Plate, waving my arms around to describe the geologic forces happening here.

"Think of the earth's crust as a spherical jigsaw puzzle," I would say, "and imagine pieces of that puzzle colliding with each other and some of them sliding underneath each other. And we are standing right at that boundary. Can you feel the earth sliding under our feet?" I would ask, as seagulls and cormorants soared high above us.

We would jump up and down to see if we could feel the plate tectonic movement. People's jaws would drop open as I told them how, if they stood there long enough, they could get sucked under. This always made them laugh.

My co-workers always teased me. They said I looked like a windmill waving my arms around like I did up on that little knoll. They could see me through the window of the visitor center. "Well, why should I just stand there and talk when I can wave my arms around and really capture their interest?" I asked.

This made them laugh even harder. "Is the arm-waving essential to give your talk when we stand in and do it for you?" they asked.

"Yes," I said, "absolutely it is."

We were each expected to learn all the talks being given, so that we could stand in for each other if someone was away. So, when it was their turn to give my talk, they tried it both ways, with and without the arm-waving. And they had to agree, the arm-waving really helped keep people's attention. As did jumping up and down, and even rolling on the ground. They all began to compete with each other to see who could give the most entertaining talk up on that hill while the rest of them watched from the little visitor center window. It got quite entertaining. Silly guys, I thought. But secretly, I was pleased. They were loving it, and so were all of our park visitors.

Tough Lessons Learned

One of our many duties as park rangers was cliff rescue. We had a lot of rock climbers coming to the area, and accidents were common. Climbing has always been a big recreational sport, but people don't always think ahead to the right outcome.

Reeve had a lot of experience with cliff rescue. Lloyd knew quite a bit about it, too, and he was a real knot-tying expert. I, on the other hand, had talents, but knot-tying was not my strong point. They patiently tried to teach me how to tie a bowline but, no matter how many times I tried, it came out wrong. I felt so dumb.

"Don't step on the rope!" we were constantly told. "You could damage the fiber and make it unsafe for cliff rescues!"

However, I managed to get reasonably comfortable with being on belay (in a rope harness with someone controlling your descent) and rappelling (stepping down a steep incline while on belay) down a cliff face. I liked leaning all the way out and being at a ninety-degree angle with the cliff. This never worried me.

What concerned me was helping injured people. I rescued countless dummies from falls and packaged them into cage-style basket litters to be hauled back up the cliff to other emergency responders waiting at the top. We practiced splinting skills, advanced first aid and CPR, and other techniques we needed to perform cliff rescue. But what if you were rescuing someone who was struggling and screaming out in pain? This worried me.

One day we were practicing with rope ascenders to climb back up a steep cliff face with an overhang, in the event that any one of us had to conduct a rescue on our own with no one to pull us back up. I understood how the equipment worked, but my boots did not have enough heel on them to properly grip the rope for the upward trip. There was an overhanging section that jutted outward and it was challenging to clamber over. Oh, how I tried to get over that obstacle! My boots would not cooperate.

I felt humiliated when my co-workers had to haul me up over that tight spot, although I managed well enough for the rest of the way. I vowed to get better at this and to get the correct footwear. Wearing the right gear makes all the difference. I would not be found lacking again.

When I went to work at a new park a year later, everyone there was impressed at how proficient I had become with moving up and down ropes. But even today, over forty years later, I still have trouble with the knots. What devious mind invented these complicated hitches? I want to hunt down those sailors for originally thinking these up and whack them over the head with a knot-tying manual.

The Marin Headlands had striking geology. Everywhere you looked there were incredibly folded and contorted rock layers crisscrossed by faults, steep ridges, and precipitous cliffs tumbling away to stunning sandy beaches below. As a student of geology from

San Francisco State University, I thought about how helpful it might be for park visitors to have a guidebook to the geology of the Marin Headlands.

I chose a route with eight numbered stops that could be easily toured by a car. There were safe pullouts along this route where the visitors could step out and examine the rock layers. I developed a booklet with hand-drawn sketches of the rock faces and described the views in engaging terms that anyone could enjoy. It really was a labor of love, and I did the majority of the work on my own time. Each sketch took ages to develop, first in pencil, and then in ink. This was long before the days of digital photography. I worked from photographic slide images to trace the initial etchings, then filled in the details by hand. I put together the blueprint booklet with text and drawings, cover, numbered pages, table of contents—in short, everything that was needed to take it to print. I titled it, *Exploring the Geology of the Marin Headlands*.

The plan was for the National Park Service to print and sell this booklet in the visitor center so that people could go out and enjoy the park geology. Everyone on staff said it was an excellent effort. Tim submitted a copy of this to the National Park Service Regional Office with a request that I receive a National Park Service Initiative Award. I kept a copy of my work for my files, but it was only a xerox copy.

The goal was for a high-ranking manager to conduct a final review of the booklet, then send it on for publication. But this never happened because, somehow, he lost it. He kept promising to find it, but he never did. And he didn't seem to care. It was gone. Lost. I was crushed. I had spent hundreds of hours painstakingly working on this booklet. Sure, I had a xerox copy, but the original drawings would all have to be redone from the beginning. It was just too much to face. I didn't have the time to do this all over again.

I received the Initiative Award several months later. It was good to have this in my file for future applications to other national parks.

But I was so disappointed that my very first effort at publication, and especially my hand drawings in ink, had been so carelessly lost by a thoughtless bureaucrat. How could someone be so irresponsible? I wondered.

I had learned a very painful lesson: never, ever give your original work to someone else for review. Give them a copy. Hand-carry your original work straight to the printer and directly supervise the production, because the moment you allow someone else to handle your hard-won effort, it may be lost.

Another tough lesson I learned was with reporters. I always liked the phrase, "Be careful what you wish for; you don't know what you'll get." There should also be a phrase, "Be careful who you talk to; you don't know who you've met."

One bright, sunny afternoon I was leading a hike up on Wolf Ridge above Rodeo Cove. This was a popular walk where I talked with park visitors about the native plants and animals in the coastal ecosystem. Our little group of about eight people had really enjoyed our time together. At the completion of the talk, two members of the group, a tall, slim, wavy-haired young man, and a young woman with long brown hair, stayed behind to ask questions. This was not unusual; most people had questions and I was happy to answer.

"Can we walk on a bit further and talk about the local bird life?" they asked.

"Sure," I said. So, I spoke about the red-tailed hawks, peregrine falcons, cormorants, pelicans, snowy egrets, great blue herons, and more. But I noticed they didn't seem too interested in birds. Instead, they kept asking questions about park housing.

"Do you live here in park housing?" they asked.

"No, I live in Pacifica, about twenty miles south of here," I responded.

"Do some staff live here? Do you wish you could live here?" they pressed.

"No, I have no need for park housing; I'm perfectly happy at home with my family," I said.

"But there are all those houses near the park entrance. Can't park employees live there?"

Now at this point, I should have become suspicious about where this conversation was heading, but it was not uncommon for people to ask about the military housing near the entrance to the park. There were many buildings there and although the military was slowly turning over these lands to the park, it was a gradual process, and only military staff lived there. I explained this to them, but they still persisted.

"If you had a choice to live here and avoid your long commute, wouldn't it be nice?" To which I firmly replied, "No, I have no need to live here." Then I abruptly changed the subject and we headed back to the ranger station. They thanked me for the talk but I felt somehow uneasy at this point. Why had they asked all those questions about park housing, I wondered? I shrugged off my concern. This wasn't the first time I'd received questions like this, although generally not so many at once.

Then the next day, it happened. I came to work and the park office was in turmoil. The entire staff was peppering me with questions and accusations.

"Why did you talk to those reporters about park housing?"

"The park superintendent is furious!"

"Why did you say that park employees should be able to move into military housing and that it is unfair to expect staff to commute to and from the park?"

I was dumbfounded. What reporters? I'd said no such thing. At first, I wasn't even sure what they were referring to, but then Tim showed me the *San Francisco Chronicle* news story falsely quoting me about park housing: "Ranger says it is unfair that park staff do not have housing with so many ex-military houses in the area ..." and so on. I was clearly named along with fake interview questions and fake answers. It could not have been further from the truth.

This was ridiculous! I tried to explain, "Those two reporters never identified themselves. I did NOT say these things, and I have never been the least bit interested in park housing."

"Well, you had better be ready to explain this to the superintendent, because he is coming out here today to speak to you in person," Tim told me.

Good grief, I thought. This was absurd. "Alright," I said. "I'll talk with him and I'll explain what happened—or in this case, what didn't happen." I was getting angry that I had been put in this position by unscrupulous reporters. "I'm going for a walk on the beach and get some air," I told Tim. "I'll be back in time to talk with the superintendent."

About an hour later the superintendent and his entourage of several underlings pulled me into the back office to "discuss my conduct." I was afraid I was going to get fired over something I'd never said. I did my best to stay calm and answer the superintendent's questions.

"Why did you talk to reporters? That's not your job."

"What right do you have to discuss park housing?"

"Is there some reason why you feel entitled to a park house?" and so on.

I was reminded again about how much this was still a man's world. I felt very small and under attack. The whole situation was patently unfair. I finally convinced them that I had been the victim of opportunistic reporters who had come with an agenda, and that I had been used as a patsy for them to air their opinions.

I had no idea how this story was generated. Those reporters had come in search of a story, but where had the idea germinated from? I had a strong suspicion the whole thing had been a setup by someone else on staff who wanted park housing to happen. But I would never know the truth.

I had learned a valuable lesson, though. Be careful what you say. Watch out for unidentified reporters. If someone starts asking a lot of questions that are off-topic, be on your guard. Ask them to identify themselves. Then direct them to the park information officer. Over the years that followed I was confronted with similar situations, but I never allowed a reporter to best me again. I was ready for them.

Bicentennial Celebration: What Happened to Our Jobs?

The year 1976 marked the 200th anniversary of our nation's official birth. A planning team came to the Marin Headlands in 1975 to begin staging the event. Music bands and big tents were going up everywhere; canvas tops and pennant flags were flapping in the wind. Crews were setting up bandstands and myriad other performance venue sites.

Large groups of people began to arrive as the events unfolded. They came from all over the country, and from all over the world. They weren't here to see the park, they wanted to see performances.

"Get out of the road with that damned horse! You're in the way of the staging trucks! Are you trying to cause an accident?" the workers would holler at us as we came around a bend on foot or on horseback.

Good grief, I thought, where did these guys come from, Hollywood? Probably, I thought. They seemed used to bossing people around. Popular trails were cordoned off, and sometimes roads were closed. Park visitors complained.

We all felt a bit overwhelmed by this. Suddenly it was entertainment versus nature, soundstages instead of seashore. Big trucks came in and set up electrical poles and satellite dishes along the narrow roads leading to the headlands and to the beach. Power cords snaked across roadways. A couple of rangers were actually thrown from their horses in the hubbub, and I worried I might be next. Traffic became congested at the key intersections. Construction workers in hard hats climbed up and down electrical poles, and everywhere there were hives of activity.

The political tenor was changing rapidly as more and more officials began to descend on the park to plan these large-scale events. Clusters of high-ranking officials gathered all around with planning maps in hand. "We could set up a bandstand here," staging officials said. Or, "Why don't we bring in some chemical toilets and set them up at this popular viewpoint?" Good grief, what an eyesore, we thought.

There was talk of expanding the Golden Gate National Recreation Area to include Angel Island, which was a California State Park, and Ocean Beach to the south, which belonged to the City of San Francisco. Plans were underway to change the whole leadership structure for the Marin Headlands.

New staff arrived to help with the increasing workload as more and more park visitors arrived. But these new employees weren't part of our original team. They had different ideas about how to do the job. Our little core group had changed, and things were no longer the same. One of the new rangers named Greg saw himself as a leader, even though he was just a rank-and-file worker like me.

"You shouldn't be out wandering the trails in the backcountry; you should be here at the office, and I'm going to talk to management about it," he said imperiously. I was completely taken aback with his audacity.

"You've no place telling me my job. I was here long before you, and we set up the guidelines together for how to manage the park," I replied.

"We'll see about that," he said.

I concluded he was an idiot and left the office to walk on the beach. We were here to talk to the public, not debate with each other behind closed doors. Our park visitors were outside, and only a very few came into the tiny little visitor center. Most people had a hard time even finding it because it blended in with all the other military buildings at the beach. Years later, the visitor center was relocated to a much larger and more prominent building on a hill, which drew lots of people.

Our schedules became increasingly regulated to respond to the influx of new visitors, and we lost our freedom to patrol where we wanted. Our close-knit core group was changing.

I began to think about working in another park and started searching for a new seasonal job. Tim had already been reassigned, Reeve was leaving for a supervisory ranger job at Stinson Beach to the north, Lloyd was given an upgrade in place to take on more responsibility, and Mick and Murray had already transferred to new assignments. Dan had left for the Ranger Intake Program in Yellowstone. Maybe it was time to move on, I thought. I had been there for two-and-a-half years. I recalled advice about how if you choose a job you love you will never have to work a day in your life. If it starts to feel like work it is time for a change of place. Those thoughts were ringing true in my head at this point.

That spring of 1975 I received an offer to work at Mount Rainier National Park in Washington State. It was a summer job, only for a few months, but it was an exciting prospect to work in such a beautiful alpine park. Assignments like this weren't that easy to come by, and this was a premier national park, one of our nation's first to be created. I could always come back to Marin Headlands in the fall or go to a winter seasonal assignment in another park.

My co-workers encouraged me to go.

"You can stay here, sure. But is it what you want?" Lloyd asked.

"We're moving on, too, except for Lloyd," Reeve said.

"A change of assignments is often a good idea, and you'll learn new skills in a new setting," Mick offered.

"I think you guys just want to get rid of me," I laughed. But I knew they were right. It was time to move on.

The Enemy!

It's funny, sometimes, the way fate sets our path for us, usually when we least expect it. I had a long commute to get to and from work in the park. I lived in Pacifica, about ten miles south of San Francisco. One evening as I was driving home from work, I stopped off at a little California state park named Thornton State Beach in Daly City, just a couple miles south of San Francisco. It was nice to break up the drive, especially after a long day at work.

A teacher from my high school days, Ron Scott, worked there, and I sometimes stopped off on the way home to say hello. But this time, when I drove up to the park, there was a different ranger in the entrance station. He had a mass of wavy, reddish blonde hair, a big man with a full red beard. He looked like Erik The Red, like a Viking. He was wearing the full California state park ranger uniform, including the Stetson hat. I was wearing my national park ranger uniform.

He took one look at me and said, "Aha, The Enemy!" This was because the national parks were trying to take over all of the state parks in the region to merge them into the growing Golden Gate National Recreation Area. So, I could hardly blame him for thinking of me as the enemy.

"I'm not your enemy," I said, and looked him right in the eye. His eyes were a deep, steely blue. I was mesmerized.

"Well then, you'd better come in and have a cup of coffee," he replied, whereupon I immediately parked my car and went in.

It was definitely love at first sight for me. His name was Vernon McHenry. He acted very friendly but official. "Where do you work and what do you do?" he asked. I told him about my job, and my background in geology. He asked if I could come by sometime and tell him more about the geology of the area where he worked.

"Sure," I said, figuring this was a lost cause. He was only interested in a science talk!

I came back a week later and talked all about the San Andreas Fault, the Franciscan Formation, continental drift, plate tectonics, and more. He acted studious and even took notes on a little pocket notepad. This is hopeless, I thought. I am totally in love and he wants to take notes about the local rocks.

I happened to meet his co-worker, Liza. She looked at me, then at Vernon, and knew exactly what was going on: two park rangers in love, and the dopey guy not knowing how to make a move. So, she invited us both to her place. Then she left us alone while she went back out to close the park. "I'll be back in about forty-five minutes," she cheerily informed us, then she went out and shut the door firmly behind her. After that nobody needed any more encouragement. We've been married since 1976.

On My Way to Washington

Early summer of 1976 saw me off on a road trip to Mount Rainier National Park in Washington State. I drove up there by myself in my blue, vintage 1962 Thunderbird. This was my first time leaving home. Up until then I had lived at home with my parents and siblings because I was still attending college. Now I was on my way to work for the summer at a new assignment in a beautiful alpine environment. I could come back to work at Marin Headlands later if I wanted to. But for now, I was off to a new adventure.

Vernon and I were engaged to be married that fall, but for now he encouraged me to go and follow my dream to work in this premier national park. "Go ahead, Babe, and don't worry," he told me. "I'll come visit you while you're there, and when you get back, we'll make a home together."

I mapped out my route and gathered up camping gear. This was a three-day trip. I packed up my Thunderbird with all my gear for the season: clothing, uniforms, a few personal items, food, and camping gear. I headed northeast through the San Francisco Bay Area to connect with Interstate 5 near Sacramento. It was exciting to be on my way. I had never gone alone on a long trip like this before, so this was a real adventure for me.

The drive was scenic, especially around the Mount Shasta region. I spent the first night at a rest stop near Redding. I had no money to stay at a motel and, anyway, I didn't mind camping outdoors. I fell asleep to the sound of trucks roaring past on the highway. The next morning, I made some coffee on my little camp stove, swallowed some cereal, and headed out. Mount Shasta looked beautiful in the morning light, and Shasta Lake glimmered a deep blue. Further north, the rugged volcanic country of the Rogue River in Oregon rolled past. I felt strong and independent.

Everything was going well until I got to Portland, Oregon. Then my car decided to stall on a terrifyingly steep, sharply curving, high bridge above a busy freeway. I thought I would have a stroke. I was so afraid. There was no place to pull over or to safely step out of the car. If someone hit me from behind, my car would careen right off the edge with me inside. My hands were shaking and my entire body was trembling in terror. I kept pumping the accelerator as the car shuddered over the crest of the bridge, until we were finally going downhill. Then I nursed the car, coughing and sputtering, to an off-ramp where I found a nearby gas station with a repair garage.

The mechanic took one look at me—I was close to tears—and immediately stopped working on the other cars to help me.

I have always been very resourceful and independent, but car trouble on a road trip ranks up there with real angst for me. The mechanic ran the car through some diagnostics and turned to me with a smile. "Your carburetor is clogged with gunk; I'll clear it out and you should be good to go." He squirted some gunk cleaner called Gumout into the carburetor while I gunned the engine, and very soon the shuddering stopped. "Here, take this can with you in case it gums up again. Just squirt this into the carburetor and you'll kick out any more junk that may be in there."

"Is that all?" I asked, incredulous.

"Yup," he said, smiling broadly.

I wanted to throw my arms around him, as visions of having to wait for days in some strange motel while my engine was repaired were mercifully dispelled from my brain. "What do I owe you?" I asked.

"Nothing," he smiled. "That Gumout can was already opened for another job, and it only took me a few minutes to clear out your carburetor. Now you can be on your way again unless you want to stay and help me change tires or work on engines." Then he laughed and let me go. I was so thankful for his help.

Back on the road again, I headed into Washington State. I thought about driving all the way to Mount Rainier, but I just wasn't sure about my car. That whole incident with the carburetor had unnerved me. This was long before the days of fuel-injected cars, and I was still feeling nervous.

I decided to drive awhile and then spend the night in a campground about an hour south of my destination. I had a sleeping bag, a pillow, a tarp to lay on the ground, a small one-burner camp stove, a little mess kit, a bag of coffee, macaroni, some rice, and cookies. It didn't take long to fix some mac and cheese and go to bed.

I was sound asleep when a ridiculous park ranger with a pinched-up expression came by and woke me up to collect fees. It was late, close to nine p.m., and I looked at him from a drowsy stupor. "Why are you collecting at this hour?" I asked.

"You have to pay your camp fees," was all he said. No one was around to collect earlier and there were no self-pay stations, so how was I supposed to do this? I got up and handed him the money, so that he would leave quickly. I never want to be like him as a park ranger, I thought before I fell asleep.

Arrival

I was up early the next morning and set out on my way again. It was cold and wet outside and I wanted to get to where I was going. I was road-weary. I headed straight for the park. I thought it would take longer to get there, but soon I could see the familiar landmarks as I got closer to the west entrance at Nisqually, on the way to Longmire. Our family had been on a camping trip here years before, so I knew the road. Tall pine trees stretched upward to the bright blue sky, the rushing river churned and cascaded downstream, emerald-green grass and avalanche lilies sprouted in profusion from the meadows, and everything, everywhere was so alive.

I felt excited to be so close to my destination. What would it be like? I knew I would live in a little cabin with three roommates. I knew I would be working full time, and I had a pretty good idea of what the job was about. But I wondered about how I would be received once I got there, and if they would mind me arriving so early. I got there about eight-thirty a.m. I drove up to cabin 136A but was reluctant to knock on the door. What if everyone was still asleep? So, I drove back down to the park office and found a supervisor.

"They won't mind if you knock on the door," he laughed. "Come on, I'll go up there with you now." I followed him back to the little cabin and he banged on the door. A young woman answered, still in her nightgown. "Your new roommate is here," he happily informed them.

I stepped gingerly inside as he roused everyone from their rooms. I felt mortified. Maybe I should have just waited in my car. A squirrel in a tree outside chittered angrily at me. "How could you bother them like this?" it seemed to be saying. But they were all very welcoming and showed me around the place. I was sharing a room with Darlene. Jill and Jenny shared the adjoining room, and Darlene's elderly friend, Hannah, was sleeping temporarily in the enclosed back porch.

We all sat for a little while in the front room to make introductions, then the supervisor headed out, leaving me alone with my new roomies.

"Would you like to unpack now?" they asked. "You get this half of the dresser drawers, these cupboards in the kitchen are yours, and you can have this shelf in the fridge." It was all very democratic and fair.

"Thanks," I said. I put some things away, but mostly I was ready to lie down and recover from the long journey.

"Get some rest; we need to go to work," they said. "Make yourself at home and, if you need anything, you can come find us around the visitor center." I laid down and fell asleep for two hours.

When I woke up, I felt disoriented. Where the heck was I? Who was I? How did I get here? Then I remembered. How long had I been asleep? I wondered. A quick look at my watch told me it was only eleven a.m. Time to get up and look around.

I wandered outside and looked around the little employee village. There were wooden cabins all over. Each was made from hand-hewn logs with little pane-glass windows. Our cabin was right at the top of the village, on the edge of the Nisqually River. I loved the sound of the water rushing past day and night. It sounded like distant voices rising and falling in a pulsing cascade. Stones tumbled along, bouncing and crashing in the opaque, silty stream.

There were trees everywhere: fir, ash, hemlock, cedar, and pine towered overhead. Alders, willow, and wild berry bushes lined the river channel. Birds flitted between the trees. Squirrels jumped along overhead and marmots peeked out from behind boulders. The adjacent bubbling springs meadow was skirted by an enchanting loop path called the Trail of the Shadows. This place was so alive—and sunny! So very unlike the lifeless, fog-shrouded suburban housing tract I lived in at home.

The next day I went to the park office to meet with my new supervisor. His name was Val. He was an older, portly gentleman who reminded me of my dad's brother, Uncle Jack. Val's kind-hearted, no-nonsense, "let's get to work and have fun" philosophy really appealed to me. He was not just a supervisor; he was also like a father to us. He made sure we were all comfortable in our lodgings, that our questions were answered, and that we each had all the resources we needed to do the job. He showed us around the visitor center and told us we would sometimes be required to help out at the front desk. But mostly, we were to be outside greeting the park visitors by giving talks, leading guided walks, and doing evening campfire programs. We were each expected to develop our own presentations, he explained. We had to create a minimum of two guided walks and two evening programs.

He took us upstairs to the park interpretive office above the Longmire Visitor Center, where we would work on developing our programs. There was a resource library and an extensive photo slide collection for giving evening programs. There were all kinds of interpretive aids and props we were free to use like animal skins, stuffed animals, artifacts, geological specimens, costumes, and so much more. It seemed daunting and exciting all at the same time.

This was an upstairs, attic-style room with open beams. The windows looked out into the lush forest all around us. If I ever dreamed of a place to work as a park ranger, this was it.

The A-frame building was constructed of heavy wooden logs in the national park service rustic style of architecture. The park administration building next door was comprised of logs and cobblestones, also with charming little pane-glass windows. Set against the conifer forest of western hemlock, red cedar, Douglas fir, and white pine, it was a beautiful place to be. In later years, the park administration staff was moved outside of the park to nearby Tahoma Woods, but back then they were right next door.

"Enjoy being here, but don't get too used to it," Val told us. "They may take it away from us at any time, or we might have this room for years—who knows? Don't rely on props or programs too much; learn your talks by heart and always have a back-up program in case the unexpected happens, which it will." The "unexpected" could be anything from a downpour, a power-outage, a wild bear attack, or other unforeseen consequences. Val was right, I came to realize. Never, ever depend on props because inevitably, things can and will change in an instant. I learned quickly to engage with my audience and let them set the tone for whatever presentations I gave.

Val was very gracious and knowledgeable. He had been with the National Park Service for more than twenty-five years. He'd seen a lot of political change over the years and constantly told us to keep our opinions to ourselves, and to come and talk to him first if we had questions or concerns about anything. As managers go, he was the best I've ever known. A rare gem. I appreciated him greatly.

Ranger Rules to Live By

RULE NUMBER 1:
KEEP YOUR TINDER DRY, AND KNOW YOUR WAY AROUND!

After we had a chance to look around the office, Val took us out to the woodshed. Are we going to get a whipping now, I wondered?

"You'll be expected to give campfire talks, so you'll need to come here before your program to pick up your firewood. I don't want to hear of a single one of you ever using more than *one match* to start your campfire," he admonished. "I've watched campfire programs all over the country, and if there is one thing that I cannot abide seeing, it's a fire that sputters out five minutes into an evening program. It's disgraceful," he told us. "You've no right to call yourselves park rangers unless you can light a fire and keep it going regardless of the weather. I don't care if it's pouring down rain. And no cheating with lighter fluid! Your fire will go out in moments and then you will look like a fool. Now, I'm going to show you how to do this correctly the first time and every time," he said. "First, you grab a piece of pitch pine. We try to always have some here for you, but keep your eyes out for more in the forest as you will always need it."

"Next, you shave off some pitch pine into slices, like this." He took a knife and peeled off some pitch from a block of pitch pine. "Then you build a log cabin fire." Val put the small pile of shaved pitch in the center and built up a square-shaped pile of kindling sticks around it. "Done correctly, this should never need more than *one match* to get your fire started," he told us sternly. "If I hear about any one of you using more than *one match*, you will be answering to me personally!" Val bellowed. "I'll find out, and you'll be held to answer. And NO PAPER!" Whereupon he looked sternly at each one of us in turn, daring us to challenge his authority on this point.

Not wanting to become the object of Val's wrath, I commenced practicing this diligently on my own. He was right, it only took one match to get a properly laid fire going. What a revelation! To this day, I pride myself on using only one match each time I light a fire. I use paper because pitch pine is hard to find when you don't live in a forest, but I never forgot what he taught us. It was a great survival tactic too.

Following our tour of the woodshed, Val asked if we had any questions. "Will we always need to come here to gather our own campfire wood?" we asked.

"You can ask your campfire talk assistant to help you with this," he answered. "If they have time to get away from their visitor center responsibilities, they're usually very happy to do firewood duty. But never assume it will be done; always check. And make sure you have enough kindling and pitch pine shavings. ONE MATCH, AND NO PAPER— REMEMBER!" We all smiled, but we knew he meant business.

With that we went about getting ready for our talks. We had two weeks to develop and memorize our evening programs.

"No reading from notes," Val warned. "Know your talk well enough to give it in your sleep." We were expected to create two different evening programs and two guided walks. I chose a guided hike to the falls, a walk around the nearby Trail of the Shadows, and a lunch hike on the nearby Rampart Ridge trail.

In between all this responsibility we were expected to learn how to answer questions at the visitor center desk, and to attend two weeks of mandatory orientation training.

"Be outside the park office tomorrow at seven thirty a.m. and bring your overnight gear for two nights. We are going on a park-wide tour and then to Ohanapecosh for orientation."

Orientation? We thought that's what Val had been giving us. Apparently, we had to learn all about the entire park. "You never know when they may need your help on the other side of the mountain," Val said. "You can't expect to just sit around here at Longmire—learn the park!"

Yikes, we all thought. So much to think about. I was beginning to think that duty at the visitor center desk all summer sounded pretty attractive.

The park tour took us up to Sunrise, and then to White River, the more remote northern side of the mountain, where we met the staff. They did a lot of wilderness and backcountry work there. I always loved the idea of working in the backcountry and becoming a backcountry ranger. It was my ideal job. Someday, I thought, I'll do this. The backcountry rangers were all law enforcement trained. I thought that sounded intriguing. And how exciting to backpack out into the wilderness and stay at one of the backcountry cabins. Oh, how I longed to do this!

We rode around the mountain and over to Ohanapecosh, or "Ohana" for short. They had a big meeting hall, and we were imprisoned there for several days learning all about park history. I felt restless sitting on a chair for days on end and was impressed by how much time and effort had been put into training us seasonal rangers. I was told that while thousands of people apply to work in national parks, only a few of us were chosen. I settled down to listen, because at that point I felt incredibly fortunate to be there.

After our time at Ohanapecosh, we returned to Longmire, stopping off at Paradise, a high mountain meadow area with breathtaking scenery. Longmire was down in a deep river valley and it was lovely. But these high meadows with verdant carpets, bright wildflowers, and shining alpine peaks were the closest thing to heaven I could imagine.

We completed the rest of our training in the big-timbered lodge hall at Longmire. We were joined by the seasonal staff from all around the park. It was great meeting everyone. Still, I was glad when it was over so we could be free to get to work and enjoy being outdoors.

RULE NUMBER 2:
YOU NEVER KNOW WHO YOU'RE TALKING TO,
SO WATCH OUT, SMOKEY!

I soon developed a guided walk to nearby Carter Falls and began leading park visitors there. We met at the trailhead and hiked uphill nearly one-and-a-half miles along the roaring river rapids, stopping to identify wildflowers and wildlife along the way. This was where I was reminded of an important lesson about speaking to park visitors: you *never* know who you are talking to. I always began every walk with first name introductions and asked people where they were from, as a matter of course. But you can never really know who you are speaking to and you should *never* assume you are in the company of strangers.

We were required to wear the full dress uniform at all times. No short sleeves. Long woolen slacks. Stetson hat. Ascot neck scarf or tie. On warm days this could be a challenge. On this particular day it was swelteringly hot and humid. I was in a sweat. I apologetically rolled up my sleeves for relief and dipped my arms into the stream as we walked upriver. The walk went well. Once we reached the falls, I told people about the area, then let them go so they could stay as long as they liked and walk back down the trail at their own pace.

I noticed that one tall man accompanied me as I started to walk back downhill. At first, I thought he just wanted to ask questions, but his initial silence alarmed me. Who was this man, and what did he want? He began by telling me it was a very good talk. Then he dropped the bomb: he was the Chief of Interpretation from the Western Regional Office.

Oh no! I thought. Now I'm busted for rolling up my sleeves. I'm sure to be fired or at least to get a terrible mark on my record.

"You should not have rolled up your sleeves and you certainly shouldn't have announced you were doing this to the group. You have a uniform code to follow and it's important to be professional at all times," he said.

"I understand," I replied, "but it's so hot today." I looked at him wearing a comfortable white cotton shirt and thought this was easy for him to say. He wasn't suffering in wool pants, a thick military press shirt, and a neck scarf and hat.

"Nonetheless, it's unprofessional to roll up your sleeves like that," he said. And he was right, of course.

"I'm very sorry. What will you do?" I asked, certain now that I was doomed.

"Nothing more," he said. "I've spoken to you and that's enough. Your talk was great and I've no intention of telling your supervisor anything. Just remember to follow the uniform rules." I thanked him and walked back to my cabin to cool off before returning to duty. I'd learned an important lesson in life: you never know who you're talking to. I remembered this from that day forward and never, ever dropped my guard like this again. I was always friendly, but I was never again *intentionally* unprofessional in any way.

Of course, even the best intentions can't always stop you from looking like a total dope. There were more idiotic mishaps still waiting for me in the wings. I strove mightily to be professional. I lit all my campfires with one match. I wore the full-dress uniform with pride. I greeted park visitors with a smile. But failure was lurking out there, silently waiting for me.

RULE NUMBER 3: DON'T TAKE YOURSELF TOO SERIOUSLY.

One day I was leading a lunch hike to Rampart Ridge. This was a popular loop walk from the valley floor up to a volcanic ridge with stunning views of jagged mountain peaks and myriad little alpine lakes. Few of the staff wanted to do this walk because it meant making a long, uphill climb along a switchback trail. But I loved it. It was a chance to get out with a small group of visitors for a nice four-hour walk. We would stop along the way to enjoy the views and then have lunch at the ridge top, where there was a stunning vista of Mount Rainier, before we clambered back down to civilization. People often bonded on this walk and there were often happy little group photos.

One day I led a special group who had signed up for the hike: a troop of Boy Scouts. There were two scout masters and a dozen boys aged ten to twelve. They were all very polite and well-behaved. The hike had gone well and we were on our way back down the hill when one of the boys asked me a funny question: "What's the most embarrassing thing that's ever happened to you since becoming a park ranger?" As fate would have it, I turned to answer and wasn't watching where I put my boots. The trail was slick and slippery from a recent rain. Suddenly my feet slid out from under me and I crash-landed right onto my butt.

There was a stunned silence. How on earth do I save face from this ridiculous blunder, I thought. My butt was covered with slimy mud. My dignity was shattered. My tailbone hurt.

I gathered my wits. "Okay, everybody, you can clap! Go ahead, it was a great fall and I want you to clap," I said. They all clapped loudly and then broke into peals of laughter. I had to laugh, too, because it was funny! Several of the boys rushed to my side to help me up. I thanked them for their gallantry and got to my feet. I almost slipped again but managed to stay upright. "Well," I said, "I guess that answers your question. This is the most embarrassing thing to happen to me as a park ranger!" Whereupon we all laughed out loud again.

I had learned Rule Number 3: Don't take yourself too seriously. We had a great walk back with a lot of laughing. Afterward, the troop leaders told me the boys would never forget this walk. I bet they'll be telling their grandchildren someday, I thought. I was probably right. My butt was sore, but I was in good spirits.

RULE NUMBER 4: NO NOTES!

Val was adamant that we never refer to notecards or notes of any kind when giving a presentation. "Know your talk so well you can give it in your sleep," he told us. "No cheating! If I see any one of you with notes you will no longer have a job here. A ranger should know in their heart what thoughts they want to convey to our park visitors. And I don't ever want to hear a recitation. No singsong voices. Tell your story naturally, like you would talk to a friend. You're not news reporters, you're not at a recital, you are naturalists, so act the part. Hundreds of candidates tried out for your jobs and you were chosen because you are the best. So *be* your best. You never know when I, or someone else from the higher ranks, may show up to evaluate your talk. You'd better be doing your best at all times. If you need to try out your talk on someone, do it with each other. Don't be too proud to accept suggestions for making it better. We can all do better, every day. I want to hear nothing but the best out there from every single one of you. I mean it!"

With that kind of a warning, we knew we had better get our lines down straight. I sat for long hours at a table going over my notes again and again. I took long walks, reciting my talks in my head, imagining what park visitors' reactions might be, imagining all kinds of possible scenarios and how I would respond to them. I knew that every talk, especially the evening campfire talks, had to be perfect. Mount Rainier was one of our oldest national parks. It had a reputation for interpretive excellence. Val was telling the truth about high expectations. I wanted not only to do well, but to excel. I wanted park visitors to be thrilled to be here. How would I achieve this? I had two-and-a-half years of experience working in the Marin Headlands, wasn't that enough? But no, this was a park with even higher expectations.

That's when I remembered the wisdom of Kirk Chance from the Hoh Rain Forest in Olympic National Park, where I had gone with my family years before. I recalled how he had filled people with a sense of wonder, and how they had followed him around, attending each and every one of his presentations. His talks were legendary. What was it about him? Sure, he looked the part, impeccably attired with shiny shoes and a Stetson hat. But it was much more than this. There was something more—he loved what he was doing. He loved sharing information about the park, and he wove this into his storytelling.

All people love hearing a story if it is well-told, and Kirk knew how to weave a story in a way that captivated his listeners. He connected with them, almost on a spiritual level. He looked at them, he listened to their questions and comments, and he bonded with them. Looking at Kirk, people wanted to learn. The learning became a shared experience. People *lived* the learning, it became a part of them, and when they walked away, they carried this experience with them. When Kirk talked about the rain forest, he communicated how it is a living, breathing entity, a part of each one of us. People were enthralled.

This was what I wanted to achieve, that deep and meaningful connection. We had all been schooled in the teachings of Freeman Tilden's Principles of Interpretation from his groundbreaking book, *Interpreting Our Heritage: Principles and Practices for Visitor Services in Parks, Museums, and Historic Places*[2]. But Kirk lived them. No amount of classroom teaching or book reading could better convey these concepts.

---

2   Freeman Tilden, *Interpreting Our Heritage: Principles and Practices for Visitor Services in Parks, Museums, and Historic Places* (Chapel Hill: The University of North Carolina Press, 1957).

Seeing "The Mountain"

When I visited Mount Rainier as a teenager with my family years before, we drove all the way around the park. We spent a week camping there, and never once saw "The Mountain," as all the locals called it, because it rained the entire time and the peak was hiding behind clouds.

Now that I was living there, I would go weeks without seeing the peak as it stayed enshrouded in misty clouds. Then one sunny day, there it would be, right in our backyard. A short walk from our little cabin up to the bridge would reward us with a spectacular view of the 14,410-foot Cascade peak, capped in snowy magnificence. Mount Rainier was named after Peter Rainier, a nineteenth century explorer, or "Tahoma," the Native American name for "The Mountain." Whatever name you gave it, it was a beautiful sight.

We were all gathered one morning in the upstairs office when a huge rainstorm broke out. Jenny couldn't contain herself—she ran to the window shouting out loud, "I love this!" I thought she was out of her mind. Who screams in delight at rainstorms? Jenny was a Washington native and loved storms.

I went to the window and looked out. It was pouring down, huge curtains of rain, a deluge! I'd never seen this much rain. The roadways were rivers of water. You could hardly see through the downpour. Thunder and lightning boomed overhead. Jenny shouted some more, until Val quietly asked her to rejoin the meeting. It was a while before she settled down as the storm roared away outside with loud exclamations of thunder.

That night the storm continued. I'd never heard such roaring and rumbling. It sounded like the whole mountain was tumbling down. BOOM! CRASH! BANG! The deafening noise made me wonder if huge boulders were crashing into the cabin. The house shook with the storm rumblings. I thought we might all be swept away by the rising river. I could hear cobbles crashing in the stream outside and envisioned a giant cedar tree falling and squashing our house.

The next morning there were downed trees everywhere. Mud and branches blanketed the roadways, almost obscuring them. The maintenance staff were hard at work with bulldozers removing all the debris. I was glad to see our little house was still standing. The river had risen during the night, but we were all safe. This was so different from anything I had ever known.

Cabin Life

Living right alongside the river in a wooden cabin had its plusses and minuses. It was wonderful to hear the sounds of the rushing river behind us, and Darlene and I often sat outside to enjoy the open air. Giant biting horseflies, an inch across, often attacked us, drawing blood where they bit. "Yeeoouch!" we would cry, as we swatted at the monstrous flies. Why were the bugs so big here? I wondered. Rivulets of blood were dripping down my leg. These are killer flies, I thought.

Our little cabin was slowly biodegrading back into the earth. Every so often the carpenter ants would swarm by the thousands and fearlessly march right across the floor of the kitchen and across the back porch. We would stomp on them, but it could be hard to stomp out hundreds at once. We called maintenance to come and spray, but the ants were always back again in a week or so. STOMP! STOMP! STOMP! How could there be so many? I wondered. Yikes! Living in the forest sure had its challenges.

It was on old place. There was an ancient oil-burning stove in the living room. It looked like a giant brown beast, three feet tall and three feet wide. Lighting it took an act of courage. You had to crouch down at the base in the back and hold a long, lighted match to the pilot light until the flame caught hold with a giant WHOOOOSH! I was always afraid it would explode and take all of us with it. A giant fireball of cabin boards and rangers roaring into the sky! It frightened us, so we each took turns doing it. But once it was lit it exuded a nice and cozy warmth like a wood fire.

On trash collection days we had to rush to cover up the bedroom windows because the trash men would always look inside to try and catch a glimpse of four young women in nightshirts.

And every so often a bat or a bird flew inside to explore the ceiling before we could collect a broom to shoo it out. "Get it, get it, get it!" we would shout as we chased these invaders out the door.

Ahhh, the adventures of living in the woods. I loved it. Every two weeks I made a long trek into Eatonville, the nearest town, to buy groceries and supplies. I would leave in the morning, make the forty-five-minute drive, shop for groceries, do laundry, stop off at the bank, and then head back. I always loved the feeling of filling up my shelves with groceries. I liked how things looked there in the cupboards, neatly organized. It gave me a great feeling of security. We each kept our own food supply, but we sometimes shared meals together. It was companionable, and I enjoyed getting to know my roommates.

Darlene was my roommate and she was a schoolteacher recovering from a broken heart. Tall, blonde, with striking blue eyes, she was brilliant, beautiful, and tough. Jenny was a glamorous brunette with long eyelashes and playful eyes that drove men wild. She was studying to be a doctor. Little Jill was a very pretty girl with long, dark, wavy hair and luminous brown eyes. Men flocked to her and followed her around.

There were no shortages of boyfriends dropping by, and I managed to convince Vernon to come up and see me every so often. I wrote to him several times a week. Back then, getting mail was a major event, and we would gaze at everyone's stacks of letters as they arrived each week. There was no internet to give us solace. Letters and word from home were what we all lived for.

I loved writing home to my family and friends about my life at Mount Rainier. I even convinced several of them to come and visit. One day, when my visiting friend, Tilly, woke in the morning, she jumped up to cover the window.

"What is that awful crashing sound?" she asked in a panic. I explained that the trash collectors came by every Monday morning. "They will want to take me away in the truck!" she shouted. "I look terrible! Cover up the windows!" We laughed and laughed at that. Even today, forty-three years later, I always chuckle to myself on trash days, remembering what she said.

Darlene eventually got some curtains to go over our bedroom windows. I guess she didn't like those guys looking in either.

Darlene was between boyfriends at the time. She had suffered a huge heartbreak a few months earlier from a man she had been engaged to. He had moved on and left her heart in shambles. She decided to throw herself into her work and was involved in a master's program to become a college professor.

And she was quick to judge. I felt somewhat at odds trying to win her favor. The more I tried, the more she shrugged me off. In some ways, it was like sharing a room with my sister, Nancy, as a kid: we often did not see eye to eye. Now here I was again, faced with a similar situation.

Finally, Darlene told me, "You try too hard to win people's approval. Stop it. Just let things come."

Hmmm I thought, I knew she was probably right. So, I backed off and quit worrying about what she thought, or what the others thought, for that matter. I wanted us to get along together and we did, so why worry about it? Later that summer Darlene remarked that I was a lot easier to live with.

"You've relaxed," she said. "That's good." I had to laugh at this—at myself.

About mid-summer, Darlene noticed that a certain young man was attending every single one of her programs. He was content to quietly attend until finally she confronted him. "What do you want?" She asked.

"To take you out on a date," he answered.

At first, she was reluctant. This man was a full head shorter than her. But then, most men were dwarfed by this striking Amazon of a woman. She asked us what we thought.

"Why not?" we all said. The guy was cute, with light blonde hair.

"But he is so much shorter than me!" she exclaimed.

"Does it matter?" Jenny asked her.

"I guess not," Darlene decided. "He sure seems to like me." Soon they were inseparable, and Stu became a part of our lives, a regular fixture at the cabin, cooking up meals for his beloved girlfriend and doting on her.

"Hey, Stu, how's it going?" we'd ask as we got home.

"Going good!" he'd answer with a big smile, as he cooked up something wonderfully aromatic on the kitchen stove.

Thankfully for me as her roommate, Darlene was a staunch Catholic and didn't want Stu sleeping in her bed, although he often slept on the living room sofa. None of us minded him being around, though, because he was such a great guy. Later that year they were married and

Darlene was broken-hearted no longer. She sent us wedding photos of her sitting in a chair and Stu standing behind her. They looked great together, and we were happy for her.

Bears and Backpacking

Every so often we would see bears wandering through Longmire Village or up at the nearby campground. Most of the time they behaved themselves and simply walked on by, acting appropriately disinterested. But every so often they decided to stick around and make trouble.

One evening we had organized a picnic with a group of ranger friends and we set up our food outside. It wasn't long before the local bears stopped by to investigate. We ran indoors and helplessly watched them tip over plates of food and drinks, carefully examining everything until they finally decided to abscond with a big bag of cookies. We went back out, cautiously, to retrieve our dinner—or what was left of it—and brought it inside to eat.

You just never knew when or where these black bears might show up. They were becoming a real nuisance in the national parks at the time. There were bear-trapping programs all over. Big barrel cans on trailers captured bears in one place, then transported and released them in remote locations. The problem was that bears are smart and always find their way back, with amazing alacrity. It would take decades of wildlife study to solve this problem. I was reminded of the childhood cartoon antics of Yogi Bear. Now here I was, seeing this for real.

Later that week I was giving a campfire program at nearby Cougar Rock when, suddenly, my group began to scream and scatter. Was it something I said? People were running in all directions, screaming, "Aaagggghhhh!" Finally, I saw the cause of the disturbance: a mother bear and two cubs nonchalantly ambling along, right through the center of the campfire circle. The mother bear kept shaking her head and bellowing, "Aruuuugghah!" as she lumbered past, her cubs in tow.

I quickly ushered people out, then hid behind the big wooden screen until the bears left. Afterward, I came back out to an empty campfire circle. Well, that's the end of that presentation, I thought, as I sadly gathered up my program materials. Silence. Total silence, where there had been bedlam just moments before. I sat down in the center of the seating area and listened to the sounds of the night: a creek rushing and gurgling nearby, my campfire crackling merrily with no one but me to enjoy it, and the stars twinkling above in the inky blackness. I laid back on one of the benches and stared up at the night sky. It was spectacular. Well, I thought, the bears had just as much right as anyone else to come to the campfire program. They had chosen to come to mine. I guess that was a good thing. It must have received a good rating from the local forest residents.

Seeing those bears made me want to get out into the backcountry. I was determined to go backpacking into the wilderness. I had my brand-new down sleeping bag, a sturdy new tent, a shiny new camp stove, my mess kit, and a little folding candle lantern.

I was all set, except that I couldn't find anyone to join me. My roomies might have come along, but they worked opposite shifts from me. I didn't know anyone else in the village well enough to invite. So, I gathered up my gear one afternoon in July and set off alone to a nearby lake. It took a couple of hours to hike in. I knew very little about backpacking and felt a bit nervous. What if a bear came, or a mad killer? Yikes! I'd read the book, *Backpacking One Step at a Time*.[3] But somehow, I felt very underqualified.

I reached the lake and set up my little camp. I looked around and saw some people on the opposite shore. Two young women. After I got all my things settled, I walked around on the lakeside trail to meet them. Best to make some friends while I'm out here all alone, I thought. But what if they didn't want a visitor? Well, I'll just have to take a chance, I figured.

"Hi," I said as I walked up to them. "How's it going?" I asked shyly.

"Great! Come sit down with us," they answered. The two women were very nice. One was a slim brunette with short hair, and the other was an elfin-looking girl with shoulder-length blonde hair. They were park employees at Sunrise, on the northeast side of the mountain, a subalpine meadow filled with kelly-green grass and a plethora of wildflowers. They were just finishing dinner and washing up their plates.

We talked about different types of backpacking equipment and I soon learned that I needed upgraded gear. They were more experienced and I noticed they had better everything than I did. The blonde girl, Bess, gave me her number and said to come visit her anytime at Sunrise. We talked for a while until the evening shadows started to fall.

Later, I walked back around the lake in the fading light, wondering if a wolf or some other wild creature would leap out from the shadows and attack me. But none came. It was peaceful and quiet. What was it like for ancestral groups of people, I wondered? Always aware of wild creatures in the darkness, it must have been difficult, yet wonderful.

---

3   Harvey Manning, *Backpacking One Step at a Time* (Seattle: The REI Press, 1973).

I heated up some noodles on my little camp stove. In this moment, I wished I could have been enjoying one of those five-course meals Mom used to make for us on our family camping trips. Here I was, all alone, eating nothing but noodles in a broth. How I wished for some of that Italian cooking right now! Mom, I appreciate your cooking, I thought, as I sat there and slurped the gelatinous-looking slop.

I climbed into my little tent and wriggled into my sleeping bag. What would I do if a bear attacked? I wondered. I had no weapon of any kind. Should I try and sleep with one eye open? Crraaack! a branch nearby dropped off a tree and banged onto the ground nearby. I jumped up.

"Hoot hoot! Hooty hoot hoot!" said an owl overhead. "Greejah greejah greejah," said the crickets. "Rribit ribit ribit," chorused the frogs. I wondered if I should be afraid. I thought a lot about bears. And cougars. Then I realized how exhausted I was and fell asleep. I slept soundly until morning.

I woke up to a shining dawn. My camp mates across the lake were already packing up. I waved to them as they departed. I heated up some water on my little stove and soon had a fresh cup of coffee in my hand. My little two-cup, aluminum coffee pot was a wonderful thing! It was cold outside, but the coffee warmed me. I fixed a bowl of instant oatmeal and was soon packing up too. It looked like a thunderstorm might be coming, and I didn't want to get caught in a downpour.

Heading back down the trail, I decided that I had really enjoyed my self-sufficiency. But I also missed the companionship of a hiking partner. I'll have to find someone to come with me next time, I thought.

Let's Go for a Spin Right into the Lake

One night I volunteered to drive and take three friends for a night out. We went to a local restaurant called The Copper Kettle, about twenty miles away. It was a great place, a log cabin shack in the woods where you could get the best fried chicken and mashed potatoes with gravy in the world. You could also buy a brand-new shiny, hand-made copper kettle there. I loved it and went there often. The food was always great and the prices were reasonable.

We all had a great time at dinner. We laughed and talked as it began to rain outside. The soft music was nice and we were having fun. Then it began to rain harder. Soon, it came crashing down in sheets. We looked out the window and decided maybe it was time to head back.

We climbed into the car. I was feeling giddy as my buddies told jokes and we laughed out loud. The road ran straight and long in the pouring rain. I didn't see the "Stop" sign until the last second. It was strategically placed in a nearly invisible location behind some tree branches.

Suddenly, I realized we were rapidly flying toward a T-intersection at the edge of a lake. I was horrified! How could I possibly stop in time? I wondered, as total terror washed over me.

I hit the brakes but the roads were slippery. As we continued toward certain death, everything seemed to shift into slow motion in my head. I saw the "Stop" sign flash past in a blur, but it was as though I could see time in milliseconds as the unfolding scene flashed past frame by frame.

My city tires were woefully unsuited for these mountain roads, and I was definitely not used to Washington rainstorms. We went into a spectacular 360-degree skid and the girls all started to holler.

"It's alright," I calmly told them as the car careened around in circles to the right, then spun into more turns to the left.

I felt like the car was totally out of control. The whole time I kept pumping the brakes to slow us down. Each time the lake went past my field of vision I was sure we would end up flying right into it. In my mind's eye, I could envision us crash-splashing into the lake and plummeting straight to the bottom for a horrible, watery death. But I knew I had to somehow reassure my terrified companions. I could not let them know I was every bit as frightened as they were.

"It's alright; don't worry," I kept telling them calmly, so they stopped hollering and believed that I had the car under control.

I watched my life pass slowly in front of my eyes, knowing I had absolutely no control at all over where the car was going. It seemed to have a mind of its own. Finally, the car skidded to a halt on the road shoulder right above the lake.

"What happened?" they all asked.

"We hit a slick patch of road on that long stretch, and the car kept going," I answered.

"Well, you did a great job controlling the car," they all said.

Controlling the car? I thought. Geez, we were lucky to be alive! We could just as easily have landed upside down in the lake and drowned. Or crashed into an oncoming car if one had been out there. It really was a miracle we had survived.

"Thanks," I calmly replied, never letting them know how terrified I'd been. I was quiet for the rest of the ride home while they continued to talk and laugh.

I kept thinking about how it would have been my fault for driving too fast in the rain. About how I was responsible for those other three, young lives in my car. After this incident I learned to respect the rain and understood how slick the roads could become in wet weather. I was beginning to realize that my T-Bird was in no way meant for winding mountain roadways.

No Brakes! She'll Be Rolling Down the Mountain When She Comes

I was really missing Vernon and finally convinced him to come visit. We arranged for him to fly into Tacoma so I could go pick him up at the airport. My roommate, Darlene, came with me and offered to drive on the way back. All went well with the airport pickup, but on the drive back, as we were descending a steep curve, Darlene calmly said, "Uhhh, the brakes are not working."

"What?" I hollered from the back seat where I was sitting with Vernon.

"The brakes ... there are no brakes," she said, as she pushed the brake pedal all the way to the floor with no effect.

"Oh my God!" I shouted as I jumped into the front seat. "Darlene, roll out of the car!"

"Roll out?" she asked, incredulous.

"Yes, tuck and roll out now, the car isn't moving that fast!" She opened the driver door and rolled out onto the pavement while I took her place and tried to stop the car.

I pumped the brakes but there was still no effect. "Vernon, Help!" I shouted, whereupon he leaped into the driver's seat and geared down the car, eventually bringing it to a halt on a flat stretch. Darlene came running down the hill to see if we were alright. "I'm so sorry! Are you alright?" I asked, looking her up and down.

"I'll be okay," she answered.

We had survived a potentially deadly crash. We were all shaking. Gradually, we gathered our wits. Thankfully, we were near an exit where we could walk to a phone and call for a tow truck.

"It's probably the master cylinder," Vern predicted. That damned car, I thought. It had almost killed us! Time to get rid of it.

Darlene was upset with me for practically pushing her out of the car. Vern was upset that I had left him in. There was no winning this. That damned car! I kept thinking.

We were all grateful to be alive. A friend came to pick us up and take us back to Longmire. The next day we had the car towed to a nearby garage where the brakes were repaired. Vern was right about it being the master cylinder. We decided he would drive the car home after his visit and sell it, then come back in two weeks with a pickup truck for me to use. Vern advertised the car in the *San Francisco Chronicle* and it sold almost immediately to a man who had a whole collection of T-Birds. He drove all the way from Los Angeles to pick it up. Good riddance, Evil Car! we thought.

For the next couple weeks I had to thumb rides from friends and neighbors, but this was not a problem. We were a small community and everyone helped each other all the time. "Just give me a list of what you need and I'll pick it up for you in town," many of them told me. What a great place to live and work.

Our roommate, Jenny, took up with a local guy named Ryan who loved the outdoors. One day he took her on a camping and fishing weekend, and they came home with a huge limit of trout. They invited our whole house to a fish fry. They rolled the fresh fish in a cornmeal batter and deep fried them. We set up a big table on the back porch so there was room for everyone. We made French fries and green salad to go with the feast. It was fantastic. I had never tasted fish so good. I don't know if it was the freshness of the fish caught that day, the cornmeal batter, the seasonings, or all of it, but it was delicious.

"I want the biggest one!" I quite rudely said, whereupon Jenny, who was serving the fish from a tray, just stopped and glared at me. "Okay, sorry," I said sheepishly, whereupon she unceremoniously slapped a trout onto my plate with a laugh.

"There's enough for everyone to have their fill," Jenny said, and that was the truth.

I couldn't believe they had caught so many fish. We all had fun talking and laughing. Jenny and Ryan told us all about their trip and how beautiful their campsite was, right near a rushing stream feeding into a lake.

Jenny was a brilliant young woman who was studying to be a doctor. We all knew that she was just doing this job for fun, and not as a career path. She had been accepted into medical school and would begin attending that fall. So, we knew this was her last summer at Mount Rainier. She was a pretty girl with dark hair, long eyelashes, and a great big flashy smile. She had learned how to use that flashing smile to charm everyone around her. She was also a no-nonsense person and she certainly had command presence. She would make an excellent doctor, I thought.

The big event of the year for the Longmire staff was Italian Night. This was always held in the big, open-timbered Lodge Hall across the river. Val lived for this event every year. He was the Grand Master of the Italian Night dinner. He spent days cooking a huge pot of delicious spaghetti sauce. He prided himself on it. He laid out antipasto, which we all helped with. There was salami, fresh home-grown tomatoes, sliced pickles, pickled vegetables, celery, carrots, peppers, ham, cheeses, olives, and more. Val arranged the antipasto on big platters in a beautiful artistic array. Everything had to be just so. There were huge bowls of green salad, homemade garlic bread, lasagna, all kinds of pasta, and fresh vegetable side dishes. Everyone contributed to the feast.

Val had us sample the sauce to see if it was up to an acceptable standard. He insisted on only using the freshest ingredients in everything. It had to be perfect. Tables were set with checkered tablecloths. There were real china plates and flatware, and real glasses for wine and water. Flowers were placed in vases, and lights were strung from the overhanging beams above. A big fire was lit in the huge stone fireplace.

We looked forward to the event all summer. Only Longmire staff were allowed to attend and we each got a ticket. We each were assigned a specific type of dish to bring to the dinner. I made homemade garlic bread with fresh French bread, minced garlic, loads of butter, grated cheese, chopped parsley, Italian seasonings, paprika, diced smoked bacon, and other toppings. It was a hit. All the food was beyond fantastic.

Several of the group played music and we all sang and laughed. We sang, drank wine, and laughed some more, until Val finally evicted us around midnight. We staggered back across the bridge holding each other upright, then continued down the roadway with flashlights guiding us to our little cabins in the woods. We clambered into our beds and fell asleep with dreams of Italian Night the next summer season.

The Short Mire Shufflers

I could hardly believe my first season at The Mountain was nearly over. I felt like I had only just arrived! It had been such a great summer, and I didn't want to leave yet. I had grown very attached to all my friends and it made me sad to think of breaking those bonds by going away. My roomies had become like family members to me, and Val was like a father.

The end of season signaled the time to develop the annual Mount Rainier seasonal staff booklet. Each area in the park was expected to develop a description of the staff and what they had achieved that summer. We were expected to choose an entertaining name for our group and to create a cartoon for the cover of our section. We brainstormed a list of names together. I suggested the name The Longmire Liars, but Jill didn't like the sound of that.

"I don't want to be called a liar, even in jest," she said.

"Okay," I said, fair enough. "How about The Short Mire Shufflers? Everyone seemed to like this name, and Jill drew a hilarious cartoon of a Stetson-clad person with long legs striding forward in an exaggerated shuffle, hands in pockets, and a fiercely determined look on their face. We all laughed aloud; it was that funny. Jill was quite a talented cartoonist.

We had a great time taking candid photos of each other doing interpretive walks and talks and describing what we had accomplished that season. Ohanapecosh, Sunrise, Paradise, and White River each developed their own sections and the whole thing was collated into a booklet. Everyone got a commemorative copy. What a great idea, I thought. A fun morale-booster and a special keepsake to take home as a souvenir of our summer season.

Before I knew it, it was time to pack up and go home. Val gave me an excellent evaluation and a letter of recommendation. He also gave me a "Highly Recommended for Rehire" rating so I could come back again the following summer. Then he gave me a big hug and said, "So long and safe travels!" I was almost in tears. This sweet man was the best manager I had ever known. He was such a great leader, so engaging, funny, knowledgeable, dedicated, yet humble in a lot of ways. He held us all to a high standard but the job was filled with encouragement and rich rewards. He had all the qualities of a leader that I wanted to emulate.

The Mountain, Season Two

After coming home that fall, I sent in my application for rehire the next summer, then waited through the winter to learn if there was a place for me. Just in case, I also applied to Lassen Volcanic National Park, as a backcountry ranger. I dreamed of doing this, working in a remote area, and staying in a little log house somewhere in the wild.

I knew I could be good at this. During my first summer at Mount Rainier, I had spoken to several of the backcountry rangers about their job duties. Basically, you had to be in excellent physical shape and go through a several-week intensive course of backcountry ranger training. It was a tough course, but I knew I could do this. I just needed to talk to the backcountry supervisor.

That fall Vernon and I were married in the little coastal village of Mendocino, California. It was a small affair with fifty guests, including my group of friends from high school, and my family. A good number of Vernon's family came too. We had our reception in the big log cabin hall at nearby Russian Gulch State Park. It was very rustic with a big stone fireplace and wooden picnic tables.

We had a catered dinner and all the guests had a wonderful time. Vern and I stayed late to acknowledge all the guests who had driven for hours to arrive there. Then we spent a night at the Mendocino Hotel, and continued on for two nights of camping at nearby Hendy Woods State Park. We camped in the back of our little old pickup truck with a camper shell on it. Pretty darn rustic, but it was all we could afford. We were dirt-poor rangers, but we were very happy.

Later that year we moved from Fort Bragg on the coast to a little state park house at Hendy Woods. I loved it there in those beautiful redwoods but was restless for something to do. I hoped I would have a summer seasonal job with the National Park Service.

Early in the spring I received a letter from the new Longmire Chief of Interpretation, Rick. He told me I had the job and that he looked forward to seeing me in May. I was thrilled to be hired back and immediately accepted. There was still no word from Lassen, but I was very happy to return to Mount Rainier. Val would still be my immediate supervisor, but Rick would oversee all we did.

When I first arrived for my second season, I was alone for a while. My roommates would not arrive for another couple of weeks. I met Rick and his family and was happy to get to know them. Val had returned and was happy to see me. We began working right away to set things up for the arriving crew. We had been given the use of the former park administration building because the administrative staff had all been moved to an office outside the park at Tahoma Woods. Now we had a much larger area to work in, which was helpful.

I cleaned up our little cabin so that when my roomies arrived, they would find a shining clean house. There was a lot to be done.

Rick told us we had to clean the restrooms for two weeks until the maintenance crew arrived. At first, I felt put off by having to do this task, but when Rick came in and cleaned right alongside of me, I was impressed. Here was a high-ranking manager taking on the task of cleaning restrooms! If he could do this with a smile on his face, then how could I think I was too high and mighty? "Get over yourself, Rose!" I told myself, as I grabbed a scrub brush and got to work. I cleaned those restrooms to shining standards. I'd had plenty of practice doing this at home.

Soon my roommates arrived. Jenny had gone off to medical school, but Darlene and Jill were back. They decided to room together so I would be with the new girl, Rita. Rita and I had written to each other that spring, as Rick had encouraged us to do, so that we would already have a rapport with each other by the time we met. This was a great idea.

I liked Rita right away but was dismayed when I realized she was my polar opposite when it came to housekeeping. I had been raised to be extremely neat and clean: a place for everything and everything in its place. Rita thought nothing of throwing everything on the floor and leaving it there indefinitely, including dirty underwear. Ugh, I thought, how on earth could I live with this? I tried to pick up after her and put things away but she did not appreciate this and told me to leave her stuff alone. Fair enough, I thought, but how to resolve this difference?

I finally just sat down and talked with her. We came up with the ingenious solution of drawing an imaginary line down the center of the room. She had one side and I had the other. My side was immaculate, swept, neat, and clean. Her side was disorderly. I did draw the line at rotten food because it attracted critters, and I would pick up and clean any food containers more than two days old, but the rest of the time I forced myself to let things be. It was a real exercise in mental discipline for me. The trials of having a roommate, I thought. But then, she probably felt the same. It was merely a matter of perspective, I guess.

My husband was equally feral. When I first met him, his house was messy with huge piles of dirty clothes and rotten food lying around, so I already had some training in dealing with this kind of situation. But at least Vernon allowed me to clean up after him, and I managed to get him to help, occasionally. With Rita it was different, and I just had to adjust. Eventually, I just blocked it out and we lived together in peace.

She made up for it by being a great friend. She had a real interest in herbal remedies and brought up a whole big box of dried herbs. She liked diagnosing illnesses and offering remedies, and she was very good at it. I developed a real interest in herbal remedies that summer. Perhaps I had drawn the lucky roommate card after all: I had a Slob Healer for my Bunkie. Teach me, oh Great One!

That spring I had worked at home on a new campfire program, A Story of Logging in the Pacific Northwest. This was inspired by a similar slide presentation Vernon had given at Hendy Woods. Hendy was a beautiful park with many heritage redwood trees. Extensive logging had occurred in the area all around the park, so Vernon's talk was really appropriate for the area. I asked him if I could use this idea for a talk at Mount Rainier, and he loaned me the books he was using.

We pulled together photos of logging in the late nineteenth and early twentieth century lumber camps, and I talked about what the life of a logger in the Pacific Northwest was like, and about all the dangers and hardships they faced. I also wove together a story about forest conservation, and how forests can be a renewable resource if they are properly managed. There were large swaths of clear-cut lands in the national forests that surrounded Mount Rainier National Park. Visitors driving in through the Nisqually entrance on the West side often became upset when they saw the logging. I explained that while some kinds of trees like cedar and hemlock need partial shade to flourish, other species like Douglas fir thrive in direct sunshine. Those broad swathes of clear-cut forests could be renewed into Douglas fir forests.

I took quotes of logger ballads and tales from the logging history books and interjected these into the slide program. Some of the quotes were so funny that people in the audience laughed out loud. "Life could be pretty grim at times in camp," I'd say, showing a photo of a bearded logger with a fierce expression on his face. "He looks pretty grim," I'd remark, whereupon the audience burst into laughter. We also sang logging camp songs throughout the program to make it an engaging interactive experience. Some visitors came up afterward and spoke of their own family history with logging and said how much they enjoyed the program.

My program assistant came up to me one night after the program and said she really liked the talk as well. This was high praise because she was a tough, no-nonsense young woman. Praise from one's peers is the highest form of encouragement, I thought. This talk might actually be worth listening to.

After I gave one of these presentations, visitors showed up at the park visitor center asking what other talks I was giving, and each week I had a little following of people who attended every program, like old friends. This was the kind of thing every interpretive ranger lives for, sharing information with a group of others who truly want to learn together. I always learned as much from them as they did from me.

That spring before I arrived at the park, I had done another bit of preseason preparatory work. I asked my Structural Geology professor if I could write a research paper on the geology of Mount Rainier for special credit. It wasn't an easy sell, because the university generally preferred to teach their own curriculum and did not usually endorse freelance studies. But because I was in the final year of my bachelor's degree program and would be working in a geologically active area, he agreed to the proposal. He said I would need to do more than just write a paper. It would have to be a comprehensive field study with rock and soil samples to be photographed, mapped, collected, and analyzed. I was fine with this, and we outlined expectations together.

I spent over one hundred hours of personal time studying the park geology papers and maps and journeying around the mountain to collect rock and soil samples. It was an excellent challenge, and I enjoyed doing it. There was no comprehensive book on park geology, so I had to do a lot of research on my own, looking up past studies that had been conducted on volcanic and glacial activity in the region.

I wrote up a booklet with maps, illustrations, and photos. When I returned to class that autumn, I cut thin sections of the rock samples I'd collected and analyzed the optical mineralogy of each. This is done by looking at the shifting light patterns of rock crystals under a microscope.

My professor was so pleased with the work, he awarded me several units of credit. "You should publish this study," he told me. At the time this seemed like a daunting prospect, but in retrospect, I wish I had done this, since this was a needed resource for the park. Entitled *A Visitor's Guide to The Geology of Mount Rainier,* I think it could have sold well in the park visitor center. But my earlier experience with a supervisor losing my work during final review, plus the time needed to fully prepare a book for publication, gave me cold feet. In the end, I thanked my professor for the special credit and let the publishing dogs lie.

Backcountry Job Offer at Lassen

I had been at The Mountain for about two weeks when the offer came in from Lassen Volcanic National Park: would I like to come and be a backcountry ranger at Juniper Lake? I would live in a backcountry cabin and conduct daily foot patrols throughout the area. There would be a lot of autonomy, although I might be needed to help out at the main visitor center with the backcountry permit program part of the time. It was an exciting prospect and I was really torn. This was the job I had always wanted, to become a backcountry ranger. The wilderness area of Lassen was beautiful with snow-covered mountain peaks, deep blue alpine lakes, and amazing geological and hydrothermal features. It would be a great adventure to work there.

But now I was already settled into my job at Mount Rainier. I didn't want to just pick up and leave. Rick was very supportive and said he would respect whichever decision I made. I did some real soul-searching but decided to stay where I was. If Lassen had called sooner things might have been different, but now I wanted to stay where I was.

I did talk to Pete, the backcountry manager at Mount Rainier, asking if there was any room for me to help with backcountry tasks that season, and to work as a backcountry ranger next year. He said he was very open to the idea of me working with him next summer, but he already had a full crew this year. No problem, I thought, that's something to look forward to in the future, at least. Little did I know at the time that I would not have another opportunity to work a backcountry job. It has remained a dream all my life.

We all had to go through pepper spray training that summer. A girl who worked the entrance station at North Cascades National Park in northern Washington had recently been attacked. We were trained how to use Mace and we were to carry it with us at all times while on duty. We weren't peace officers, but management wanted us to have a way to defend ourselves if we ever found ourselves in a bad situation. It made me think about how important it was for each of us to always be on our guard.

Most park visitors were kind, and they came to the park with a true love of the outdoors. But there were always a few who might be dangerous, and each of us had to be on the alert for negative behavior. We were told that, if at any time we felt threatened, to leave the program without delay, return to park headquarters, and immediately report the situation.

Someday I am going to be a full-time law enforcement ranger, I thought. I wanted to be able to defend myself and others, and to protect the park resources from harm. Years later, a young woman was working at Yosemite National Park when she was brutally attacked and killed. Before it happened, she had repeatedly expressed her concerns about the remoteness of the location where she was assigned. She was a naturalist with no law enforcement training and she was a clear target for an attack. Someone should have listened to her concerns and addressed her situation. Instead, she lost her life. It was a terrible tragedy. Three other women were attacked and killed at a motel just outside the park. Eventually, the killer was brought to justice, but it made me aware of just how vulnerable women could be.

I never wanted to find myself in a situation where I couldn't defend myself, so I was constantly on my guard. I was always friendly, but I made sure I kept everyone at arm's length and did not walk or talk alone with strangers. The 1970s were a decade of serial killers, and we all understood how important it was to be on the alert.

I began to notice some unusual changes in myself that summer. I suddenly seemed to have a natural aversion to coffee and alcohol when I had always wanted these before. I had put on a little bit of weight, which puzzled me. This was a new and upsetting series of developments which I could not explain. What was wrong with me, I wondered? Maybe it was age; I was over twenty-one now and getting on in years, I thought. I had no clue, figuring it must be hormonal, so I just shrugged it all off and focused on the job.

Mountaineering Adventures

We were all required to learn basic climbing and mountaineering skills that season. I was pretty comfortable with the rappelling and using rope ascenders to pull myself back up. I really enjoyed it and, apparently, I did so well the local reporters took photos of me and posted them in a news article about park ranger training. This was validation for me after failing so miserably at climbing skills in Marin Headlands the year before. My cabinmates asked how I learned so fast, and I told them I had previous training.

"Wait until tomorrow when they take us up into the snow," Jenny said.

Hmmm, I wondered, what would they do to us there? I had zero experience in alpine mountaineering. Would I slide downhill into an abyss? Fall into the dark depths of a glacial crevasse, to disappear forever?

The next day we met in the big hall and went over the basics of mountaineering: how to rope up together, how to look out for each other, and most importantly, how to stop our fall with an ice ax if we should begin to slide downhill. This all sounded good in theory, but it was much more difficult in practice.

We were each equipped with thick canvas gloves, rain parkas, knee pads, a helmet, and an ice ax. Our instructor took us to the top of a steep incline. "Your ice ax can save your life," he told us. "Never go mountaineering without it, because it might be the only thing saving you from a potentially deadly fall. Now watch me as I fall and swing my weight around while leaning on my ice ax. This is a critical skill and you are all going to have several opportunities to practice this." Then he leaped forward, threw himself into a downhill slide, reached out with his ice ax and rolled over onto it as his body careened downhill. He put his head down and dug into the snow with the tip of the ice ax. He slid a good twenty or thirty feet before he came to a stop. "You see," he shouted up to us, "all you have to do is dig in hard with your ax and then throw your weight onto it so you can grind to a halt. Now you try it, one by one. I'll stay down here to make sure you all land safely."

One by one we tried it. It was exhilarating to fly forward, slide fast, roll onto your stomach, and clasp your ax hard into the snow. It was also amazing to see how much force gravity exerted, and how hard you had to dig the ax into the snow to stop your slide downward. Some of the others slipped and ended up on their backs, unable to stop their momentum until gravity brought them to a halt. But everyone learned quickly.

We got back later that evening, sore and exhausted. It had been a good day and one which I never would forget. I can still feel the metallic hardness of that ice ax under my chest, digging into the ice and snow.

After our mountaineering training, Jill decided she wanted to climb to the peak of Mount Rainier's 14,410-foot summit. We were all offered the chance to do this with park climbing guides. It was considered on-the-job training. I considered it but decided that I preferred to keep to the slopes below the snow fields. I felt no need to scramble and slide in freezing ice and snow, just to get to the top. I never did understand the need to climb to the tops of mountain peaks, although I respected people who did this. I was happy to look at mountaintops from the comfort of the forest and meadows below.

But Jill really wanted to go. She set her alarm for an ungodly hour every morning for a month so she could complete her physical readiness training. Darlene was her roommate and every time that alarm went off, she groaned, "Get out of bed, Jill. No snoozing! If you're going to wake us all up with that damned alarm, then get up." Yikes, I thought. Darlene could be fearsome, but I had to agree with her.

Jill was determined, though. She ran, exercised, did circuit training, stretched, and generally got into great shape. She lost ten pounds. We were all impressed. "Join me," she said.

"No thanks," we all chorused. We were content to sleep in and enjoy our morning coffee from the cozy comfort of our happy little cabin. Having nothing but a thin sheet of nylon tenting between us and the outside world in freezing arctic cold held no appeal for the rest of us.

Finally, the day came for the climb, and Jill was off on her multiday adventure. Her backpack was ready. She had a notebook with pens and envelopes. What for? we asked.

"I'm going to write to you while I'm on the trip," she said. "Halfway up is a posting place where you can drop letters, and fellow climbers will carry them down for you on their way back." Amazing, I thought.

Sure enough, the next day we got a letter from Jill. She told us how much she missed all of us. She talked about how difficult the journey was, and thanked Darlene for supporting her during all those early morning awakenings. She drew little sketches of the scenery and funny drawings of her "dead underpants" and of her campmates in exhaustion at the end of the day, which made us laugh out loud. It struck me just how close we had all become as friends, that she would take the time to tell us how much she missed us after one day.

Jill was an incredibly sweet spirit. She came back three days later sunburned, exhausted, blistered, and elated. She told us how life-changing this climb was for her, and how it had been so incredibly beautiful up there on the top of the world. I never forgot her journey and what it had meant to her—and to all of us.

Mount Rainier was ringed by big, long glaciers. One trail led straight to the base of a glacier. This was the Kautz Creek Nature Trail, where a huge swath of volcanic mud had cascaded down the Nisqually River in a raging torrent, knocking everything out of its path several years before. Hot gas had vented out of the ground near the side of the glacier and immediately turned ice into water, mud, and rocks. This deadly mudflow knocked over thousands of trees like toothpicks, devastating everything in its path for miles. Over the years a trail was created leading to the base of the glacier where the mudflow had emerged.

This trail provided an unusual opportunity to walk directly up to the base of a glacier. Deep blue ice, huge crevasses, and monstrous ice walls greeted hikers who ventured up this trail. I was mesmerized by the desolate beauty of it all. I walked right onto the ice field, careful to stay on the trail. With one false step a hiker could fall into a deep, cavernous crevasse and be lost. The base of the glacier was brown with dirt, but further up the ice looked transparent where daylight filtered through, creating prisms of color. It was stunningly beautiful.

For many years, park visitors came to see the ice caves on the side of the mountain near the Paradise Visitor Center. Each summer the snow would melt enough for people to go into these deep blue passages and explore the inside of the glacier. But with the advent of global warming, the ice caves vanished.

Even in the 1970s climate changes were happening rapidly. Glaciers had already begun retreating all over the world. So, to be able to walk up to the toe of such a massive ice field was a real adventure. I had no idea it would all be so breathtaking. And so alive. You could hear the water pouring off the sides of the glacier, down into the river, which roared out of the bottom. Giant creaking and popping sounds boomed all around, a music of the earth. It was as if the earth was talking in a deep, melodic timbre. I could feel it reverberating through me, a deep connection to the planet. This beautiful planet. Our Earth.

Fire Team

I wasn't going to work as a backcountry ranger that season, but I did have an exciting side duty: Forest Fire Suppression Team. There had been a prolonged drought during the mid-1970s and the fire danger was extremely high. Park staff was asked to help the U.S. Forest Service fire teams and be on fire standby. Those of us who wanted to train for this duty had to pass a physical fitness test and be able to run a mile and a half in eleven minutes, forty seconds.

I was a good hiker but not much of a runner at the time. I barely managed to complete the run in the prescribed time, but I passed. For some reason, I was having more and more trouble keeping up with things. I was continuing to put on weight, and I tired easily. This puzzled me.

We attended a week of fire suppression training in the adjacent U.S. Forest Service camp. Afterward, we were required to keep a go bag packed and ready at all times. If a wildfire broke out, we would be airlifted to the fire and sent straight into action. I was incredibly excited about doing this. A couple of times I was nearly called out, but the call was canceled at the last minute because the local teams managed to put out the fires quickly. Damn, I thought. I really wanted to go. But my call never came.

My little go bag sat there forlornly in a corner of my room, mocking me with its stillness. Maybe I should start jogging, I thought to myself. My gut was continuing to bulge out, but it was a firm kind of bulge, not sloppy fat. Could I be pregnant? I wondered. But no, that was impossible. I had taken birth control pills every day for years. My monthly cycles were irregular and often completely absent due to the high concentration of estrogen in the pills. So missed periods meant nothing to me; I'd had no period in ages.

As far as I was concerned, I was not expecting. There was a small amount of movement in my belly, but I shrugged it off as indigestion. I decided I was getting out of shape and that I needed to get more exercise. So, I started hiking harder, farther, more and more uphill. I worked myself into excellent shape. I firmed up all over, but that gut persisted. Must be the long-term weight gain of being on the pill for years, I figured.

All during the summer I seemed to be drawn to little children. I had taken care of kids ever since I was eleven years old, when I began babysitting. But for some reason, now I found children more interesting. I made a point to talk with them. I remember Val telling us that when we wanted to talk to children to get down on their level. Squat down or sit down so that you were eye to eye and show genuine interest. Never talk down to children, just talk with them. Share information with them like you are telling a story. Ask them questions. Listen to what they have to say. Reply with thoughtful answers. Pay attention. Kids loved this, having a park ranger get down on their level.

I soon put together a children's program. I met the kids in the campground and brought a day pack with me. Inside the pack were all the things a hiker would want to have with them. I would ask the kids what they would bring in their packs.

"Cookies!" they often said, or "Chocolate bars," or "My teddy bear or dolly."

"Those are all good things to bring," I said, "but let's talk about some other things you might like to have with you." And I would take the items out of my pack and put them on a table for everyone to examine, water bottle, healthy snacks, mini first aid kit, rain parka, wool cap, flashlight, whistle, and so on. Pretty soon I had a group of visitors of all ages listening in as they gathered around and asked questions.

"What should I take on a backpacking trip?" "Should I bring a portable toilet?" "How about a battery-powered coffee grinder?" and so on.

A good children's program always attracted visitors of all ages. Darlene and Jill had put together a program on backpacking which they gave on the steps of the visitor center. It was well-attended too. They even took out their backpacking stoves and cooked a meal. What a great idea!

One and One is Three

Then one day in early September, I went with a group of co-workers for a day trip to swim at nearby Morton Lake. At one point I went out into the water to swim. But for some reason, my whole lower body cramped up and it was suddenly extremely hard for me to move. One of the guys saw me struggling and swam over with a floatie ring. He towed me back to shore.

"Are you alright?" he asked, looking at me with worry.

"Yes, thank you," I replied, wondering what the heck had just happened. I felt so embarrassed. Why had I cramped up like that? I went and sat on shore, waiting for the others to finish their fun, and feeling left out. On the ride back home, I kept wondering what I had done to cause the cramping. I was fine now, but it had happened so unexpectedly.

When I returned to my cabin, I undressed and looked in the big mirror in the bedroom. I was all alone in the house. I hadn't really looked at myself undressed for weeks and weeks. I looked closely, like I hadn't done before. I saw that my navel was completely pushed out. My stomach was a hard, firm, raised mound. It couldn't be! Oh geez, I thought. I *am* pregnant!

I couldn't believe it. I had been so busy all summer long I had ignored all the signs. No morning sickness, no indigestion, and I was running up and down trails every day. I felt just fine. How could anyone be so dumb as to overlook a pregnancy? I must have been in denial all summer long.

I looked up the name of a local doctor and made an appointment the next day to confirm my discovery. He was really kind. He walked into the exam room, put his stethoscope to my navel, and listened for a moment. Then he handed the stethoscope to me: "Would you like to listen to the heartbeat?" he asked.

Oh my, the heartbeat! "How pregnant am I?" I asked in alarm. It was September.

"I would say you are due around Christmas," he said.

What? I was in complete shock.

"You didn't know?" he asked, incredulous.

"No," I said. "I thought it was latent symptoms from being on the pill for so long. And I'm tall, so I don't show much."

"You are very slim," he agreed. "You don't look five to six months pregnant. I guess there's enough room for the baby to stand up in there." He smiled.

"What will I tell my husband?" I wondered out loud.

"You're married?" he asked. "Then, congratulations are in order!" he laughed.

I slowly drove back to the cabin. I went to bed early and spent that whole night just staring at the wall. I was in shock. How had this happened? I guessed it was because I had stopped taking birth control pills right before I left home. I thought I had a grace period before the missed estrogen dose wore off. I'd been taking the pill for so long I really didn't think missing one day would matter. How many new parents could echo this same thought? I wondered. Well, apparently, I had figured wrong.

I called Vernon to tell him the news. He was very supportive. "Don't worry, Babe. It's great news! We'll be fine. Just relax. I kind of thought you were pregnant when I saw you earlier, but you were so sure you were just putting on weight from the pill, so I kept my thoughts to myself. Well, I see now that I was right. I'm going to be a father!"

I was so grateful to him for how he took the sudden news. I hadn't been sure what to expect. Then I called home to my mother. "Mom, guess what you are going to be for Christmas?" I asked her.

"Do you mean what am I going to get for Christmas?" she asked.

"Well, that too," I said.

"What are you talking about, Honey?"

"You're going to be a grandmother for Christmas," I said. Now my mom still had my little seven-year-old sister, Chrisi, at home, so she was in shock too.

"What?" she asked incredulously. She couldn't believe it.

I talked to my roommates the next day. They were amazed. How could someone be several months pregnant and not know it? they asked.

"Well, look at me," I answered. "How pregnant do I look to you now?"

Not much, they all agreed. And yet here I was, five to six months along, and none of them had noticed.

"Well, it will be a very short pregnancy then," Darlene said.

Good point, I thought.

Then I went over to tell Val about it. He was remarkably kind. He could see I was shaken. I told him about staring at the wall all the night before.

"Well, there's nothing to see there," he said. "No point at all in staring at the wall. Do you want to go home?"

"No," I said. "I am fine to keep working until departure time, but I'd better quit the fire team. I guess it was a good thing I never got called." Indeed, the universe had been looking out for me. Smoke inhalation, extreme heat, and intensive physical work might have caused a miscarriage.

"Okay," Val said, and put a fatherly arm around my shoulders. I put my head on his shoulder and he pulled me into a big bear hug. "Why don't you come home with Myrna (his wife) and me tonight? We live in Tacoma and you can stay in the guest bedroom. It will give you time to absorb all this and you can relax there, away from everything." It was an incredibly generous offer, and it sounded very appealing to me.

"Alright, I will. And thank you, Val."

"Not to worry, Rosanne, everything will be alright."

That afternoon I talked with Darlene about going to Val and Myrna's house. She said it would be a good time for me. She had been a guest at their home several times and she loved Val and Myrna.

"They will make you feel completely at home, like you are their family." They had two grown children who had long since moved out, so there was plenty of spare room for guests.

That evening Val, Myrna, and I were off to Tacoma. They had a nice, comfortable home and they managed to set my mind at ease. "Just relax, and don't worry about anything," they told me. They cooked delicious meals. I was able to get some much-needed sleep. They were more than kind, like family. By the time they brought me back to Longmire, I was so grateful to them for taking care of me. It was a kindness I never forgot.

One afternoon about a week later, I was walking along the Trail of the Shadows near the Longmire Visitor Center. I didn't know if my unborn child was a girl or a boy, but in my mind, I kept seeing a little blonde girl. I was thinking of names. I wanted a name that was different. Then I saw a mother with a little girl walking up the trail. The girl was blonde and soft spoken. I squatted down so I was at eye level with her. I think she may have been three or four years old. "What's your name?" I asked her.

She whispered something I could barely hear. "Her name's Cameron," her mom said, and smiled.

"Hello, Cameron, how are you? What do you like most about the park?" I asked her. She loved the trees and seeing the snow on The Mountain. She said she loved running down the trails and climbing into the trees. I told her how happy I was to meet her and asked to shake her hand. She was a sweetie, and I thanked her and her mother for coming to the park. I said goodbye and reminded them to come to the ranger programs if they had time. Then I walked down the trail and thought how much I loved that name. I talked to Vernon a couple days later and asked him if he would like that name if we had a girl. He said it sounded just great to him.

As the initial shock of my pregnancy wore off, I began to look forward to the birth of our child. I really had no idea if it would be a boy or girl because back then, there was no common technology to determine the sex of the child. But I kept seeing that little blonde-headed girl in my thoughts, and I really looked forward to meeting her.

I would have to ramp up quickly once I got home to get the nursery prepared, and to get onto regular prenatal care. But I wasn't worried because I was in the best physical shape of my life. I had been hiking up and down trails every day and I felt great.

Of course, this would mean a real change in my life with Vernon. We wouldn't be able to just take off on impromptu little camping trips after the baby was born. We would need to wait until the baby had grown a little older, and then maybe we could go out together on trips.

But we did have a big road trip planned to go to Bryce Canyon National Park, Zion National Park, and Grand Canyon National Park that fall after I returned home. I wanted to backpack down to the bottom of the Grand Canyon again. I had done this a few years before on a geology field trip and I wasn't going to let a pregnancy stop me. I knew I could do it and I looked forward to this big trip, and to the later trips we would take as a family with our new child.

Pregnancy is not an illness, it is a natural way of life, I had heard many times. Too often, American women stopped strenuous physical activity and treated pregnancy as a waiting condition. Then they fell out of shape. I wasn't going to let this happen to me. I saw no reason to slow down, and I began to look forward to our new life as a family together.

I did not look pregnant and, except for my roommates and Val, no one else noticed the changes in me. I kept wearing the same uniform and although it was a bit tight, it served me fine until I left that autumn. I am tall, so there was plenty of room for the baby to move around inside. And she did, constantly. I figured she was probably going to be an athlete someday. This made me smile.

Sing Along

I don't sing well. In fact, I'm terrible at singing. But one of our responsibilities was to lead a weekly sing-along evening program in the big-timbered community hall at Longmire. "Can't I just do a campfire program, instead?" I asked.

"Nope," Val said. Many of our park visitors were annual returnees who had been coming every summer for decades, and they looked forward to the community feel of the sing-along. Good grief, I thought, what would I do?

"Just put together a list of songs and let them sing for themselves," Darlene told me.

"But someone needs to get them started, someone who can carry a tune, right?" I asked.

"It doesn't matter," she told me. "All you need to do is get them started."

"Easy for you to say; you can actually sing," I said.

"Buck up," she said. "You'll do just fine."

Right, I thought. Buck up, don't F*** up! Sheesh. I felt like an idiot just thinking about how I was going to do this ridiculous thing.

There was no organized format, no preprinted songs or anything. It was up to me to choose whichever folk songs I wanted, so long as they were traditional American songs. So, I chose some old favorites, like *She'll be Coming Around the Mountain When She Comes, Down in the Valley*, and so on. I typed them up and printed them out, making copies. I memorized all the words and tried singing to myself. I sound like a jackass, I thought. This was going to be a disaster.

The night of the sing-along ominously approached. I seriously considered calling in sick, but I was pretty sure if I did this that Val would be at my bedside with a spoonful of cough syrup, checking my temperature, and catching me in my lie. There was simply no way out of the dilemma. Repeated entreaties to my roomies to stand in for me fell on deaf ears. Time to buck up, I decided. Maybe the audience would be as tone deaf as I was. Fat chance.

The evening of the event I opened the doors to the community hall early. Maybe no one would come, I fervently hoped. But to my dismay they came in droves, practically knocking down the door, filling up the hall, and taking up every available seat. There must have been more than 300 people. Omigosh, I thought, this was going to be a huge disaster! And there was nowhere to hide. There I'd be, a total fool in front of a big gathering, trying to do my job and looking like an idiot in the process. Maybe there was still time to quit my job.

I greeted people and handed out copies of the songs. "You'll need to share with each other," I told everyone, but they didn't seem to mind. Everyone looked so happy. I looked longingly at the back door, thinking maybe no one would miss me if I left. Nope, they were all looking at me expectantly.

I smiled and welcomed everyone. I told a few Native American legends, which people always enjoyed. I had spoken to local Native American elders to gather genuine stories from them. The last thing I wanted was to be called out for phony storytelling. "Clueless Park Ranger Tells Farcical Tales at Local Sing Along" was the headline I feared.

After a few stories, someone said out loud, "Excuse me, ranger. Are we here for storytelling or a singalong?" My time was up and there would be no more stalling.

"Okay, folks," I said. "I have a confession to make. I can't sing. But maybe you can help me. I can start the songs but then you have to drown me out with all your voices right away, okay? Otherwise, you are all going to be very sorry if you have to listen to me make a fool of myself." There was dead silence for a few seconds. Uh oh, I thought. Now I've really blown it. Then everyone in the room burst out laughing. I mean they were laughing so hard they were almost crying. People acted as if they had never heard anything so funny. And the funny thing was, I had been dead serious, yet there they all were, laughing out loud. "Okay," I said, "I guess that's a yes." More uproarious laughter.

"She's so funny!" I heard a guy in the front row tell his wife. They were all smiling and ready.

So, I started with the first few notes of a song and, thankfully, the group took over. Every song. I hardly had time to feel tone deaf before they were off and running with every tune. They were all singing and clapping and before I knew it, the program was over. Afterward they all came up and thanked me and said they had loved it. I figured they were probably lying, but I thanked them for their kindness. I was immensely relieved, for them as well as for myself.

The next day Darlene overheard a smart aleck teenage boy talking about how he felt like he had been to a "hootenanny" the night before, because the park ranger made everyone clap and sing. "What did you do to those poor people?" she jokingly asked me.

"I guess I tortured them," I replied.

Fan Mail

The next day there was a note for me pinned to the community bulletin board. It was from someone named Danny, asking if I would write to him. Who in the world was this, I wondered? I didn't remember anyone named Danny. I took the note back and showed it to my roommates.

"You have a mystery admirer!" they all laughed.

How could I find out who this was? Darlene suggested I simply write and tell him how my week was going and casually ask him about himself. "You could say, 'I led two walks to Carter Falls and gave three campfire talks and went to the store and talked to my friends, and oh by the way, who are you?'"

We laughed pretty hard at this. I just could not figure it out. This wasn't like Darlene's boyfriend, Stu, where he had come on all her talks and then finally asked her out. This was far more mysterious. This person seemed to know who I was and wanted me to stay in touch. Was this appropriate?

"Write back and see what happens," she said. "You don't want to be rude and not reply to a park visitor."

I did not want to encourage unwanted admirers, but decided to answer, more out of duty than anything else. I was a little bit curious too. So, I replied and thanked him for writing. I told him about my week. Then I asked him to help me remember who he was. I asked which of my programs he had been to. And I thanked him again for writing. Then I mailed it off to the address he left with the note.

A week later I got a letter. It was written in a child's hand. I opened it up and a photo of a sweet-looking little boy dropped out of the envelope. He said he had been to my campfire talk, the walk to Carter Falls, and the sing-along. He said he had spoken to me at the visitor center too, and that he went on a walk with me around the Trail of the Shadows. He said his whole family had stayed at the park for a week and that he really enjoyed all of my talks. "Now do you remember me?" he asked.

It was so sweet, I had never before or since received a letter quite like this. I wrote back and told him how much I appreciated his coming on all my presentations. I asked him about his life and what he loved doing. He wrote back several times that summer. He asked me to call him once, so I did. His high little voice sounded shy and sweet. I thought how it would be so nice to have my own little boy someday.

Many years later, when I was working at Death Valley National Park in California, there was a little girl named Robyn who also came on all my talks and wrote to me afterward. Her older sister, Linnea, was also a treasure. Their family stayed a week and got to know all of the ranger staff. These are the moments that remind us why we are alive, I thought. To make a difference in the life of another, and especially a little child. To help them feel the wonder of the great outdoors and our rich natural heritage. These are the moments that made me proud to be a national park ranger.

The author at Death Valley National Park in March, 2011
with Robyn and Linnea Goh

Going Home

After the demise of my T-Bird with the brake failure incident, Vernon had brought up a mini pickup truck with a camper shell on it. Now that summer was ending and autumn leaves were turning gold, it was time to head home. Days were shorter and much cooler, and snow would soon start to fall in the weeks ahead. I had stayed on well into September, and now Vern wanted me to come home so we could go on our road trip to the deserts of the Southwest. The Grand Canyon, Zion, and Bryce Canyon awaited us. I was starting to show, and my uniforms were getting pretty tight by then. We had only a few months left before our first child would arrive.

We had plans to backpack down to the bottom of the Grand Canyon. We wanted to see the river narrows at Zion and to hike to the top of Angels Landing. We would camp right out of our little mini pickup. I was really looking forward to the trip.

It was time to head back. Soon we would be a little family. I packed up all my things, hugged my cabinmates, and told them goodbye. I knew I would really miss everyone, and that I would miss being a park ranger. As I headed west out of the park with The Mountain in my rearview mirror, I realized that a whole new part of my life was ahead of me. I was happy to be going home again.

I also realized that I had become a park ranger because of all the wonderful trips my parents had taken us on during my childhood. I thought back over the many years our family had spent time together in so many beautiful places, and how these trips had shaped me— had shaped my future. Sometimes our adventures together had been wondrous, other times nearly disastrous. These experiences had been fun, funny, exciting, educational, thrilling, joyous, silly, heartbreaking, entertaining, and above all, amazing. Always amazing. It was during these wild and special moments that I felt such a love for the natural world, and a desire to share that with others.

I knew there would be more park ranger jobs in my future. My experiences at Golden Gate National Recreation Area and Mount Rainier National Park were only the beginning. I dreamed of the future and the new adventures it would bring.

I smiled all the way home. This is what I was born to do.

The End

Join the author soon in her upcoming book, *Trip Tales Two: Travels with Gus*, where she describes all new family adventures in her tiny, cantankerous little camper named Gus. Laugh with her as she finds herself in even wilder challenges as a California state park ranger. River rafting patrol, mountain bike rescues, wildfire suppression, and the U.S. National and World Gold Panning Championships are just a few of the many adventures in store.

Visit www.TripTalesBook.com to get updates.

Acknowledgments

There are many people to thank for helping me to make this book the best it could be. First of all, a huge thank you to my patient, kind, and helpful husband Vernon McHenry who encouraged me to write this story and had so many great suggestions for how to make it read well.

Thank you to my family including my daughter Cameron McHenry, my son Tristan McHenry, and my sister-in-law Jeane Fleck for reviewing and offering very useful feedback. Thank you to my friends Jan Chapralis, Karen Ho, Tricia Slattery, and Kari Koskinen for their excellent reviews and remarks. Robin, Cas, Joanie, Charly, and Anita—thank you, too, for reading the early chapters, and for all your encouragement.

My sister Chrisi Vargas was a huge supporter with all of her encouraging words and for contributing her own memories to the stories in the book. Many thanks also to my brother, Gary Smith, for his helpful comments, support, and encouragement. We laughed a lot at all the stories over the years. A special acknowledgement to my little sister, Nancy, whom we miss every day..

Thanks to Dr. Ronald M. Callender, Barbara Moritsch, JoAnn Levy, Dianne Milliard, Susan McLaughlin, Kitty Williamson, Mike Lynch, and Genevieve Parker Hill, for their very insightful, thoughtful and kind endorsements of this book.

My gratitude to Dr. Denzil Verardo for not only endorsing this book, but also for his comprehensive, perceptive, and gracious Foreword. It is an honor to have known him throughout the course of my park career.

A thank you to Jordan Fisher Smith for many helpful suggestions about how to get published, and for guiding me on who to speak to for help with this book project.

Thanks to Tricia Gardner, her husband Steven Goh and their daughters Linnea and Robyn Goh for allowing me to use the photo of the girls with me at Death Valley National Park.

Thank you to Janica Smith and her publishing group who patiently helped me bring this book from a manuscript to a published work. Without them, this book would not exist! They include Heidi L. Eliason, my kind and incredibly patient editor, Yvonne Parks at PearCreative.ca for her beautiful cover design and book layout, Clarisa Marcee for the final proofread, and Russell Santana for the index.

And of course, many thanks to each of the characters in this book, all of whom are very real and who helped to shape my life in so many ways.

Thanks to my Mom, Flora, and my Dad, Carroll, the best parents any kid could ever hope to have! Dad: thanks for instilling a love of the outdoors into us. Mom: thanks for all your dedicated love and caring. Thank you both for taking us on all those trips to wild places.

Index